2025

SUN SIGN

BOOK

Forecasts by

Claire Comstock-Gay

Copyright © 2024 Llewellyn Worldwide Ltd. All rights reserved.
ISBN: 978-0-7387-7199-1
Cover design by Kevin R. Brown
gettyimages.com/130224825/©KateDemianov
gettyimages.com/1390852567/©ulimi
gettyimages.com/1441253474/©calvindexter

Published by Llewellyn Worldwide LTD
2143 Wooddale Drive
Woodbury MN 55123

Printed in China

Contents

Introduction

Welcome to the 2025 edition of *Llewellyn's Sun Sign Book*! This book offers a road map to your year ahead, from the major adventures and big-picture changes to the ups and downs of everyday life. This is an especially exciting year astrologically, as Pluto, the planet of transformation—which stays in each sign for up to thirty years at a time!—finally moves for good from pragmatic Capricorn into idealistic, rebellious Aquarius.

What does Pluto's entrance into Aquarius mean for *you*? Well, that depends. Every astrological event, from the most fleeting Moon phase to the long-lasting movements of the outer planets, affects each of us differently. We're all different people, after all! But your own Sun sign—that is, the zodiac sign the Sun was in at the moment of your birth—can offer not only insight into your personality, but also a more targeted picture of your year ahead.

In this book, you'll find descriptions of each sign, overall forecasts for your year ahead, and monthly forecasts that include noteworthy astrological events, New and Full Moons, and a few days that are likely to be especially rewarding or challenging for you. These forecasts won't cover every single thing that might happen in 2025—astrology isn't one-size-fits-all, and you're much more than just your Sun sign. (You have a

Moon sign, Mercury sign, Venus sign, and more!) If you're looking for specific information, a personal reading tailored to your unique birth chart is your best bet. But if you're looking for some general guidance for your year ahead, you just might be surprised at how useful a Sun sign forecast can be.

What you *won't* find in this book are pie-in-the-sky promises, dire warnings, or lists of ironclad dos and don'ts. Think of this not as a book of rules you have to follow, but as a helpful guide to the astrological landscape you're about to move through in 2025. Some of it will be lovely and exciting, and some of it may be stressful, but the outcomes aren't written in stone. Astrology is about possibilities, and it's up to *you* to decide what you'll do with them.

Claire Comstock-Gay writes weekly horoscopes for *New York* magazine's The Cut and is the author of *Madame Clairevoyant's Guide to the Stars*. She lives in Minneapolis, MN. Visit her at ClaireComstockGay.com.

2025 Sun Sign Forecasts

by Claire Comstock-Gay

♈

Aries

The Ram
March 20 to April 20

Element: Fire
Ruling planet: Mars
Keyword: Initiative
Key phrase: I am

Gemstone: Diamond
Power stones: Bloodstone, carnelian, ruby
Color: Red
Flower: Geranium

All about Aries

Strengths and Gifts

The Sun enters Aries each year on the spring equinox: this is the start of a fresh cycle and brand-new astrological year. You're the first sign of the zodiac, Aries, and you have the personality to match! You're all about taking initiative, starting new projects, and charging forward to chase your dreams.

This pioneering spirit is one of your key strengths. If you see something you want, you don't waste time pining, and you don't wait until you have a perfect plan before taking action. (After all, conditions are *never* totally ideal.) Instead, you simply dive in, trusting that each step will lead to the next one, and that, if nothing else, your sheer force of will can carry you through.

Some people hesitate to make the first move—they're scared of looking silly, of being the first one to try something, of moving forward without a guide to lead the way. Not you. If anything, you *are* the guide. You're not afraid to take the lead, and you'll show everyone who follows you how it's done.

You're probably incredibly skilled in your field—not just because of innate talent, but because you have the confidence to chase your dreams. You're not someone to back down from a challenge! You understand that you'll never get what you want if you aren't brave enough to try, so you don't tend to hold back or settle for less: you go for it.

Wishy-washy people likely frustrate you, because you can't quite understand where they're coming from. You know how to make decisions, and you know how to do it confidently and *quickly*. It's not (necessarily!) that you're being reckless, only that you're able to keep your eyes on the prize. You don't get lost in mazes of hypotheticals and what-ifs. You simply act.

Finally, for better or worse (but mostly for better!), you're a straight shooter. You say what you mean, and say it with your chest. Friends don't have to worry about where they stand with you: they *know*. If you have doubts about a project at work, you'll share them. If you find a new crush incredibly charming, you'll say so! Though your personality can be fiery, you're not one to get caught up in drama or games. You say what you mean. More people could stand to follow your example!

Friendship and Love

When it comes to relationships—both romantic and platonic—your mantra is *shoot your shot*. No deep unspoken passion for you, no secret unrequited longing, no hanging back because you're not sure if the person you just met wants to be friends or not. That's just not how you operate. If you like someone, you make your move! Whether that means asking your crush out to drinks, laying down some heavy flirting, or straight-up asking that new person whether they want to be more than friends, you go for it. If they say no, they say no—there are plenty of fish in the sea, and you'll have moved on by tomorrow. (After all, you love the thrill of the chase and might even get bored when things are too easy!)

This confidence is immensely attractive! While you might sometimes worry that you're a bit *too much*, the truth is that people probably respond incredibly well to your passion, fire, and fun. (It doesn't hurt that Aries is ruled by Mars, planet of lust!)

You're allergic to games and manipulation—you don't pull that with others, and you won't tolerate it when others try to mess you around. When it comes to you, Aries, what you see is what you get. Your friends and lovers won't ever have to wonder whether you're upset with them—they trust that you'll say something! You're straightforward about how you feel (even when that's ill-advised). This also means that you don't really do grudges, which can be a bit disconcerting to some of the more brooding signs. Being up-front about your feelings—even when you're a bit explosive about it—means that you're able to get over things quickly.

The flip side of this is that you sometimes struggle when others *aren't* so straightforward with you. You're open and honest with others, and you expect honesty in return, so it's challenging when people play their cards close to their chest. Sometimes you could use a reminder that just because others don't express love in the same way that you do, that doesn't mean they don't feel it.

Work and Money

While nobody loves being micromanaged at work, you chafe more than most. Your decisiveness is one of your greatest strengths, after all, so it's maddening when you aren't given the space to actually use it. Workplaces with lots of rules and bureaucracy likely aren't going to be the best fit for you. You need the latitude to make choices and *act*. When you have it, that's when you can truly excel.

When it comes to money, your philosophy probably sounds something like: what's the point of having it if you're not going to use it? In other words, cash tends to fly out of your pocket! You love an impulse buy: if you see something you really love, you'll splash out right then and there (forget about saving up or waiting for a bargain). You're incredibly generous with what you have. To you, treating your friends is one of life's greatest pleasures. But when it comes to finances, you aren't the most long-term thinker and may need a bit of encouragement to focus on saving for the future.

Struggles and Growth

Every sign has its weaknesses—it's nothing to be ashamed of! For you, Aries, the dark side of your wonderful confidence and decisiveness is recklessness. You make choices *quickly*—but not always wisely. You're not someone who naturally tends to think ahead, which has its benefits (you live in the moment!) but can also get you into trouble. If you can learn to slow down just a hair, think before you speak, or maybe get a second opinion from a friend before you charge forward, it'll save you from all kinds of headaches down the road.

The other big potential problem area for you is your temper! This, of course, is the flip side of your famous passion. It's easy for you to step on toes and hurt your friends' feelings without meaning to. Words said in the heat of the moment can still *hurt*, and can cause lasting damage to your relationships.

Journaling Page

Think about your goals for 2025. Which of your Aries gifts—confidence, decisiveness, willpower, initiative—will you call on to help you achieve them? Which elements of the Aries personality do you want to lean into this year?

The Year Ahead for Aries

The Eclipses

Eclipses are major drivers in the story of your year, and 2025 has four of them: two lunar and two solar, in Virgo, Aries, and Pisces. Each of these eclipses marks a period of big, likely unexpected change, and while they affect everyone, they're particularly potent when they connect with important points in your own astrological chart.

This year's first eclipse, a lunar eclipse in Virgo, comes on March 14th. With the Moon in your solar sixth house, health issues might come to your attention: take care during this period to listen to your body. Maybe you've been taking your health for granted or pushing yourself too hard—we all do sometimes! But this is a good time to notice what's out of alignment and take concrete steps to treat yourself with more care.

Two weeks later, a solar eclipse in Aries (and your solar first house) happens on March 29th. You've been through the wringer over the past few years, with eclipses in your sign in both 2023 and 2024. Each one has probably highlighted a change in your relationship with yourself: What makes you happy and fulfilled? What gives you confidence? The answers might surprise you. This eclipse will likely present emotional challenges, but ultimately it's an opportunity for you to grow. And take heart: this is the last Aries eclipse until 2032!

Then on September 7th, the second eclipse season of the year kicks off with a lunar eclipse in Pisces. This one's likely to stir up major emotions for you, and there's a good chance you'll come to some surprising realizations about yourself. Make a point of being extra gentle with yourself.

Finally, September 21st brings the final eclipse of 2025. Under this solar eclipse in Virgo, you can expect your daily habits and routines to be shaken up. Try not to be rigid! If you're flexible and adaptable, you just might discover new (and even better) systems for organizing your life.

The Big Picture

While the personal planets (Sun, Moon, Mercury, Venus, and Mars) serve as guides to your personality and day-to-day life, the outer planets of Jupiter, Saturn, Uranus, Neptune, and Pluto tend to be best for charting the themes, phases, and overarching story of your life.

Headline news for you, this year, is that **Saturn** and **Neptune** are both still moving through Pisces and your solar twelfth house. Some people find twelfth-house transits to be tough—this is the domain of solitude, secrets, and life-changing inner work—but they can also be spiritual and deeply rewarding. Saturn's been moving through your solar twelfth house since 2023, stirring up big feelings about past failures (real or imagined) and existential questions about your place in the universe.

You've been reevaluating your goals and accomplishments in preparation for a brand-new phase of life. Neptune's been moving through this same house since 2011, sparking an interest in the spiritual side of life, but possibly making you struggle with feelings of purposelessness. It's heavy work! You have probably had some major revelations and are feeling more than ready to wrap up this chapter and move on to the next. While you're not *quite* there yet, this year you'll see light at the end of the tunnel as both planets pop into Aries (and your solar first house) for part of the year! Neptune enters Aries on March 30th before moving back into Pisces on October 22nd, and Saturn enters Aries on May 24th, moving back into Pisces again on September 1st. Think of these periods as previews of a bright, bold, idealistic period to come.

Jupiter, planet of luck and abundance, begins 2025 in Gemini (and your solar third house of learning, communicating, and socializing), and stays there for about half the year. This is a time to focus on learning, meeting new people, and broadening your social circle. You really never know where an interesting conversation might take you or what kinds of opportunities a chance encounter could open up! Jupiter enters Cancer and your solar fourth house on June 9th, where it'll be for the rest of 2025. During this second half of the year (and particularly during an absolutely lovely Jupiter-Venus conjunction on August 12th), shift your focus from making new friends to deepening your relationships with old ones. This is a time for putting down roots: if you've been wanting to move to a new apartment or buy a house, chances are good that you'll finally find the perfect spot after Jupiter moves into Cancer.

Unpredictable **Uranus** continues on its six-year journey through Taurus and your solar second house, which began in May 2018. Expect continued shake-ups in the realm of money and finances—both for you personally and for the world at large. It sounds scary, but it's not all bad: Uranus can cause trouble, but it can also bring amazing unexpected opportunities. The key is to stay open to the unknown and not to hold on too tight to any one outcome. Know that change is inevitable—and ideally be ready with a plan B—and you'll be well equipped to weather this storm.

Finally, intense and faraway **Pluto** spends all year in Aquarius and your solar eleventh house, where it'll remain until 2043. If this Pluto transit is making an aspect to one of the planets in your natal chart—for instance, if you have other planets in Aquarius—then you'll experience this transit more intensely. Otherwise, Pluto's effects tend to be felt societally more than personally. While it's in idealistic and technology-minded Aquarius, expect movements for social justice around the world to pick up steam, and AI to become even more of a hot topic.

Your Ruling Planet

As an Aries, you're ruled by Mars, the planet of action! Just don't expect the start of this year to be action-packed, as Mars begins the year retrograde in Leo and your solar fifth house of fun and self-expression. You'll likely experience a false start or two as Mars moves backward through the zodiac, asking you to reevaluate your relationship to your ego. How do you want to be seen by others? What role do you want to play in your social circle? What needs to change for you to feel more like *you*? (During this period, you might decide to change up your look with a dramatically different hairstyle or a fresh tattoo, but don't schedule your appointment until *after* Mars retrograde ends on February 23rd.) During Mars retrograde, everything will move much more slowly than you'd probably prefer. Think of this period as a chance to build your skills and confidence before the real action begins. Once Mars stations direct on February 23rd, it's all systems go!

January

The year gets off to a slower start than you'd probably like! Luck planet Jupiter is retrograde in your solar third house all month, asking you to be extra thoughtful about what information you're taking in (and sharing!). For now, reflection is enough: the time for action comes later. More urgently, perhaps, your ruling planet Mars is retrograde all month long: expect everything (especially your sex life) to be a little wonky and unpredictable, so do your best to take things *slow*.

Moon Cycles

The first Full Moon of 2025 falls on the 13th in Cancer and your solar fourth house of home and family. You might experience family drama or personal breakthroughs about what *you* need to feel secure. Schedule some time for quiet, personal reflection.

The first New Moon of the year comes on the 29th. This New Moon, in Aquarius and your solar eleventh house, is a time to set intentions based on your unique individuality. Don't automatically do what others are expecting of you: stay true to yourself.

Power Days

On the 10th, others might be surprisingly generous with you: accept the gifts that come your way with grace! On the 19th, your creative juices will be flowing, so make the most of it. On the 25th, you have an opportunity to heal an old wound and finally get closure.

Days to Watch For

On the 6th, expect hidden tensions in your life to rise to the surface and demand your attention. On the 7th, you may be more irritable than usual: be careful not to take it out on people you love! On the 15th, others may try to push you around, so be prepared to stand up for what you believe in.

February

If you felt directionless, insecure, or unlucky during the first month of the year, you should feel things start to turn around for you. Jupiter retrograde ends early in the morning on the 4th, and—even better—Mars retrograde ends the night of the 23nd. After Mars stations direct, *no* planets are retrograde for the rest of the month—ideal conditions for moving forward and setting plans in motion. On top of that, Venus enters Aries early on the 4th, and the Sun joins it on the 18th.

Moon Cycles

The Leo Full Moon arrives on the 12th, in your solar fifth house of self-expression, creativity, and play. This might be a deeply romantic—and potentially dramatic—Full Moon for you. It's also an excellent time to write, paint, dance—to express yourself in whatever way feels right.

It's followed by a New Moon in Pisces (and your solar twelfth house of spirituality and secrets) on the 27th. Under this Moon, you're likely to be extra perceptive, but also extra sensitive. Don't push yourself too hard: what you need right now is gentleness.

Power Days

The 6th is an ideal day for socializing: no drama, just fun and good vibes. On the 10th, the conditions are right for romance: this could mean meeting someone new, asking out your crush, or planning a date night with your partner. On the 20th, your charm will be at its peak, so ask for what you really want.

Days to Watch For

On the 3rd, you might say something you don't mean in the heat of the moment, but it's never too late to apologize. On the 15th, insecurities may arise, especially in relationships, so treat yourself with extra kindness. On the 24th, past dramas might reignite: do your best to avoid falling back into old patterns.

March

In addition to this month's eclipses (more below), this is a big month for you! Three planets enter Aries this month: Mercury on the 3rd, the Sun on the 20th, and Neptune on the 30th. With so many planets in your solar first house, get ready to enjoy your moment in the spotlight! However, Venus retrograde begins on the 1st, followed by Mercury retrograde on the 15th. Don't expect totally smooth sailing (especially in the romance department), but don't worry too much either: a little introspection and care will go a *long* way.

Moon Cycles

On the 14th, the lunar eclipse in Virgo activates your solar sixth house. This eclipse is likely to highlight areas in your life—especially relating to your job or health—where things aren't quite right. Don't ignore what you're feeling: let this powerful lunar energy motivate you to make a necessary change.

Then March 29th brings a solar eclipse in Aries: expect to feel the effects (but also reap the benefits!) especially intensely. Eclipses bring the change we didn't even know we needed, and this one might open the door to an era of fresh confidence and self-love.

Power Days

The energy on the 5th is super sweet. If you put yourself out there, you might meet someone special. The 24th is a great day to strengthen your bond with a new friend. On the 28th, your intuition is supercharged: trust your gut, even if it doesn't make logical sense right now.

Days to Watch For

On the 2nd, reckless decisions could lead to unwanted consequences, so extra caution is warranted. On the 8th, even the strongest relationships might be put to the test—but with care and compromise, you'll be fine. The 22nd might be one of those days when *everything* feels frustrating: venting to a trusted friend will help a lot.

April

Good news: those retrogrades from March are ending this month! Mercury stations direct on the 7th, followed by Venus on the 12th. Both of them moved backward into Pisces for a short time before returning to Aries this month: Mercury on the 16th and Venus on the 30th. As both planets retrace their steps, you might feel a sense of déjà vu: try to see this less as a frustration and more as an opportunity. If you wish you had done things differently during Mercury or Venus retrograde, you just might get a second chance now.

Moon Cycles

The Full Moon in Libra arrives on the 12th, lighting up your solar seventh house of partnership. If you've been experiencing conflict, this Moon might signal a breakthrough. If you've been seeking love, you could finally find what you want (or, just as importantly, realize what you *don't* want).

Then there is a New Moon in Taurus and your solar second house on the 27th. This New Moon is a major opportunity to reset your relationship with finances: if you've been stressed out about money, this is a prime opportunity to create a new budget or a debt repayment plan.

Power Days

On the 7th, you'll have the confidence and inner balance needed to make solid decisions. On the 15th, bold and imaginative strategies might be more successful than following the rules. The 25th is a day for big emotions: be honest about how you're feeling, and your relationships will grow deeper than ever.

Days to Watch For

On the 4th, you may finally have to deal with any frustrating tasks or difficult conversations you've been avoiding. Moodiness will ramp up on the 10th, so just focus on staying grounded. On the 26th, you might feel extra insecure: spend time with people who make you feel loved for who you are.

May

On the 4th, Pluto begins its five-month retrograde in Aquarius and your solar eleventh house: you may experience major shake-ups in communities you belong to. The Sun and Mercury both move into Gemini and your solar third house of communication this month (the Sun on the 20th, Mercury on the 25th), so be prepared for lots of socializing. On the 24th, Saturn enters Aries (where it hasn't been since 1999!): your confidence levels might dip temporarily as you face new challenges, but ultimately you'll learn big lessons about who you are and what you want.

Moon Cycles

On the 12th, a Full Moon in Scorpio and your solar eighth house could be a sign of intense experiences to come—or general dissatisfaction with anything boring or shallow. We all need to feel real passion sometimes, and this Moon might help you find it.

On the 26th, a New Moon in Gemini and your solar third house is a time to be guided by your curiosity. Ask questions (without assuming you already know the answers!), and you'll gain important wisdom about yourself, your relationships, and what you really want from life.

Power Days

If you've been saving up to splurge on something fancy, the 3rd could be the time to finally go for it. Your brain is firing on all cylinders on the 5th: this is an ideal time to make big plans. The 22nd is one of the best days possible for love *and* lust: get out there and enjoy yourself.

Days to Watch For

On the 2nd, it's *incredibly* easy to ignore red flags, especially in new relationships: get advice from someone you trust. On the 8th, others may try to convince you to settle for less than you deserve: don't listen! The 28th may bring feelings of loneliness, so treat yourself to something nice. You deserve it.

June

On June 6th, Venus leaves Aries and enters Taurus. Chances are good that you'll find excellent financial opportunities coming your way—but it's also extremely easy to spend unwisely, so be mindful of your budget! Mercury and the Sun both move into Cancer this month (Mercury on the 8th and the Sun on the 20th): use this time to grow closer to or mend fences with family or old friends. When Mars, your ruling planet, enters Virgo on the 17th, you'll likely find that putting your energy toward helping others ends up benefiting *you*, too.

Moon Cycles

If you've had questions or doubts lately about your purpose in life, the Full Moon in Sagittarius on the 11th may provide answers. You might meet someone exciting and new or be offered an opportunity to make major changes. At the very least, you can hope to find clarity.

The New Moon in Cancer (and your solar fourth house) on the 25th is an invitation to begin a new cycle. Spending quality time now with your loved ones—or just yourself—can set the scene for gentler, more nurturing, more rewarding relationships in the days ahead.

Power Days

The 4th is an amazing day for socializing: focus on friends (but if you're looking, stay open to finding something more). Your smarts and drive are at their peak on the 5th: take on a challenging new project. If you've been struggling to choose between multiple options, the 27th is a good day to make your final decision.

Days to Watch For

On the 9th, misunderstandings are everywhere: try to save important conversations for another day. On the 15th, tension may arise between yourself and your loved ones, but patience and communication will go far to alleviate any drama or hurt feelings. On the 18th, you're unlikely to be thinking clearly: sleep on any big decisions.

July

This month's headline news is that unpredictable Uranus enters Gemini on the 7th after more than six years in Taurus. The way you socialize, communicate, and connect with others may change—likely because of new technology, new ideas, or new people in your life. Three planets station retrograde this month: Neptune on the 4th, Saturn on the 13th, and Mercury on the 18th. While Mercury moves backward through Leo, creative projects in particular may seem to fizzle out. Discouraging as it may feel, this isn't the time to give up. Keep at it and you'll ultimately be glad you persisted.

Moon Cycles

On the 10th, a Full Moon in Capricorn could mark the culmination of a long-term professional project—or long-simmering feelings about your career path could reach a climax. Now might be the time to bring one chapter to a close, so that you can begin a new one.

On the 24th, a New Moon in Leo asks you to honor your creative side. Think about what would make your life feel more exciting, more enchanting, more vibrant, and commit to making time or space for that in the days and weeks to come.

Power Days

On the 6th, you'll have the opportunity to truly help your friends out—and to strengthen your bond while you're at it. Go with your gut on the 15th: impulsive moves will likely lead to grand adventures (or at least some good fun!). On the 24th, your intuition is heightened, so trust yourself.

Days to Watch For

On the 9th, you might feel deep dissatisfaction with your life, but avoid the temptation to blame others: it'll only make you feel worse. On the 19th, insecurities are activated, but working through them will help you grow. Avoid scheduling dates on the 23rd (and if you're on the apps, consider taking the day off!).

August

Moon Cycles

On the 9th, a Full Moon in Aquarius suggests that drama in your community or friend group may finally come to a head. This is your chance to clear the air, express your feelings, and make things right—or move on.

On the 23rd, a New Moon in Virgo is a good time to set fresh intentions to get organized, take care of tasks you've been putting off, or fix problems you've been avoiding. (Just be careful that you're not resolving to change or "fix" other people!)

Power Days

Be bold on the 11th: calculated risks are likely to pay off. In both your career and your personal life, you can trust that the universe has your back on the 13th. On the 25th, think long-term: make romantic commitments or invest in high-quality items that are made to last.

Days to Watch For

On the 1st, relationships (especially with family) will be under a lot of pressure: keep a cool head and take a break if you need to. The 8th may bring a challenging confrontation with a best friend or business partner. On the 22nd, don't cling to relationships that don't even make you happy.

September

On the 1st, Saturn (which is retrograde until late November) leaves Aries and moves backward into Pisces. If you've felt anxious or inadequate lately, this will likely bring some relief—and it's a good thing, since this month will bring the last two of 2025's four eclipses! Both Mercury and the Sun enter Libra this month: Mercury on the 18th and the Sun on the 22nd. This is your solar seventh house of partnership, close friendship, and marriage, so expect these themes, and questions or decisions related to them, to pop up again and again.

Moon Cycles

On the 7th, the lunar eclipse in Pisces will heighten your sensitivities, so treat yourself gently: this is no time to be tough. A deep, honest, emotional conversation with someone you trust—whether that's a partner, friend, or therapist—could truly change your life.

On the 21st, the solar eclipse in Virgo asks you to consider not just *what* you want, but also *how* you're going to get there. You may suddenly decide that it's time to totally change up your habits and routines—just wait a couple days before you do anything too drastic.

Power Days

Be assertive on the 5th! Others (especially current or potential partners) will respond well to confidence. On the 8th, you may experience an instant connection with someone new and exciting. On the 26th, connecting with others on a deeper level will clarify your own purpose in life.

Days to Watch For

If you're cranky and short-tempered on the 9th, caring for your body will help your emotions calm down. Insecurity may cause problems on the 16th, but encouragement from a family member or partner will be surprisingly healing. On the 19th, be cautious in new relationships: it's easy to get the wrong idea about people now.

October

This month, the Sun and Mercury join Mars in Scorpio and your solar eighth house. Eighth-house transits sometimes get a bad reputation, but the reality is that they're not necessarily scary, just intense. While this house is activated—especially between the 22nd and 29th—expect meaningful encounters, probing conversations, and personal transformation, whether dramatic or subtle. (Sex is often exciting, passionate, and deeply fulfilling under this influence—just don't let the thrill of it make you forget or ignore your own boundaries.)

Moon Cycles

Under the Aries Full Moon on the 6th, it's all about *you*. In other words, it's a time to get back in touch with your own personality, preferences, and emotional needs. If you've been unsure of what you want or how you really feel, this Moon will bring clarity.

After the personal insights revealed by the Full Moon, the Libra New Moon on the 21st invites you to reset your relationships with others—particularly partners, lovers, and close friends. If something has felt out of alignment, this is your opportunity to find a balance again.

Power Days

On the 5th, don't be afraid to break with tradition! New ideas will bring the best results. The 11th is an amazing day for social activities, especially introducing a new partner to your friends. You're likely to be attractive—practically magnetic—on the 19th! Just be careful that your ego doesn't get you into trouble.

Days to Watch For

On the 7th, simple misunderstandings could cause deeper relationship problems. Don't look for someone to blame: focus on getting to the truth. On the 13th, you may discover that a crush who *seemed* perfect wasn't who you thought. On the 23rd, a stressful family situation may ultimately help you grow.

November

November will be shaped by a Mercury retrograde that lasts most of the month—from the 9th to the 29th. As with all Mercury retrogrades, the key will be to *slow down*, double-check your work, and try to keep a good attitude if misunderstandings arise. Mercury retrograde often disrupts travel, and since this one spends time in your solar ninth house, the effect may be particularly pronounced for you. If you're booking a trip, especially for the Thanksgiving holiday, build in lots of room for delays (and get to the airport *early*!).

Moon Cycles

On the 5th, a Full Moon in Taurus could be an indicator of changes in your money situation—likely for the better, especially if you've been making financial moves this year. Avoid making big purchases, but don't be surprised if beautiful or meaningful objects seem to fall into your lap!

On the 20th, a New Moon in Scorpio is an opportunity for a transformative fresh start. If you've felt bored with your life as it is, or like you somehow aren't on the right path in life, this New Moon is a day to meditate on what you *really* want.

Power Days

On the 2nd, be prepared for surprises—the good kind! If you're dealing with any kind of complicated money situation—especially one involving shared bills—the 22nd is a great day for getting it sorted. On the 30th, breaking from your usual routines will make you feel happy, balanced, and fully alive.

Days to Watch For

On the 4th, self-righteousness—whether in you or in someone else—may get in the way of open communication. On the 9th, you may be forced to work through painful emotions related to your family. On the 15th, doubts could cause you to reevaluate your path in life.

December

On the 10th, Neptune retrograde ends, and the planet of dreams and spirituality begins moving forward again in Pisces. If you've felt some compassion fatigue over the past months, you may feel your heart softening again, or you may simply notice a sense of magic return to your life. Three planets enter Capricorn this month: Mars (on the 15th), the Sun (on the 21st), and Venus (on the 24th). This could be a good time to negotiate a promotion or apply for an award: keep an eye out for opportunities to be recognized for your work.

Moon Cycles

On the 4th, a Full Moon in Gemini is likely to bring new people into your orbit. This is more likely to be a time for broadening your social circle than deepening any particular relationship: under this Moon, even a casual acquaintance or crush could end up changing your life.

On the 19th, a New Moon in Sagittarius asks you to think about whether you need more excitement in your life. You've already achieved so much, but now you risk becoming bored. Rest and regroup—and think about what your next adventure might be.

Power Days

The 6th is excellent for making plans related to home and family life, from small things (DIY projects) to big (adding a new member to the family). On the 9th, you're so charming that you'll get practically anything you ask for. (Don't let it go to your head!) On the 14th, you can finally put old feelings to rest.

Days to Watch For

The 1st could bring confusion or emotional turmoil: focus on treating people right and you'll get through it. On the 7th, your family's expectations of you might feel particularly stressful: spend time with friends who appreciate you as you are. On the 24th, you may find that an exciting opportunity really was too good to be true.

Taurus

The Bull
April 20 to May 21

Element: Earth
Ruling planet: Venus
Keyword: Strength
Key phrase: I persevere

Gemstone: Emerald
Power stones: Diamond, blue lace agate, rose quartz
Color: Green
Flower: Violet

All about Taurus

Strengths and Gifts

Taurus is the second sign of the astrological year and the first earth sign, following on the heels of passionate (but sometimes reckless and quick-tempered) Aries. As an earth sign named after the strong bull, you're steady, determined, and dependable. You're all about creating comfort and stability—and then enjoying the fruits of your labor.

Your tenacity is one of the best things about you. You have faith that you can solve virtually any problem by slowly, steadily chipping away at it. You know that you don't need to wait around for a bolt of inspiration or a lucky break; you just need to *keep going*. While others might lose heart at the first sign of trouble, you're not so easily discouraged.

This steady determination often translates to a quiet, unshakable confidence in yourself. Once you've made up your mind, it's hard (sometimes impossible!) to sway you. Good luck to anybody who tries to pressure you to do something or to change your mind. In fact, you often truly shine when you get the opportunity to show others that they can't push you around.

You're likely a creature of habit (at least to a certain extent), excellent at creating routines and sticking to them. You treasure your daily habits and rituals, whether that means making coffee a certain way, going to the gym on a regular schedule, or calling your best friend every day. For you, there's a time and place for adventures and surprises, but in the day-to-day, you feel most confident and supported when you have a solid structure in place.

Because of this, you prefer being around those who are a stabilizing presence in your life. People who are too flighty or unpredictable often stress you out! For the most part, you choose the joys of rootedness and security over the uncertainty of wild spontaneity (though there are exceptions to every rule!).

But none of this means that you're an "all work, no play" type of person: Taurus is deeply attuned to the world's material pleasures, and part of the reason you work so hard is so that you can luxuriate in the good things in life at the end of the day. You love to surround yourself with beautiful things and quality materials. From delicious meals to soft fabrics to a cozy living space, you value the good life!

Friendship and Love

Taurus is ruled by Venus, the planet of love, and this influence makes you tremendously appealing to others (even when you don't realize it). Your appreciation of the good things in life makes you amazing at planning dates (you probably know where to find the best restaurants or see the breathtaking sunsets) and picking out thoughtful gifts.

Physical compatibility is particularly important in your relationships. This doesn't necessarily mean *sexual* compatibility (though it might!); rather, it means that touch of all kinds is important to you, and you probably need a certain amount of physical affection to feel truly happy.

In both romance *and* friendship, you're incredibly loyal. You aren't one to rush things or jump in and out of flings with just anybody: you take relationships seriously. Once you've decided to let someone into your life, you'll stand by them through thick or thin. If you had to choose, you'd rather have a small circle of people you genuinely trust than a huge collection of casual acquaintances. And as much as you love the thrill of a new relationship, what you want most is to feel secure. In order to be genuinely happy with someone, you need to trust that they're as devoted to you as you are to them, that they'll be there through thick and thin. You're not interested in a relationship with someone who can't commit, who keeps you guessing about how they feel, or who involves you in endless drama. You're steadfast and loving, and you want the same in return.

But to some people (especially air and fire signs!), your loyalty might feel more like possessiveness—even when you don't intend it that way. Likewise, if a partner or good friend has a strong independent streak or a busy social life outside of you, you may feel neglected or insecure—even if there's really nothing to worry about. In both cases, the key is simply to *communicate clearly* about what you need. Don't let the problem simmer!

Work and Money

At work, you're dedicated and reliable. While some people prefer to work in short bursts or sprints, you prefer a steadier approach. Chaotic workplaces likely won't be the best fit for you, though in some cases you can bring some much-needed stability to such environments. For the most part, though, you shine brightest when you can simply put your head down and do the actual work you were hired for. While you're a hard worker, you're not one to make your job your entire life: you love your leisure time *far* too much for that.

Money is very important to you, not necessarily for its own sake, but because of what it can buy. You care about your creature comforts! This could mean that you want a luxury car, designer clothes, a lavish house—or it could mean that you love hunting for high-quality pieces at the thrift store, then going home to your cozy apartment that's decorated just how you like it. You value money because of the comforts and luxuries—whatever those words mean *to you*—it can offer.

Struggles and Growth

Your tenacity is practically a superpower—it lets you get things done, stand up for yourself, and stay true to your values. The trouble is that when taken to the extreme, it can turn into a stubbornness verging on rigidity. Refusing to be pushed around is one thing, but refusing to compromise at *all* can end up damaging relationships—or getting in the way of your own personal growth. If you can learn to let others get their way every once in a while—or even come up with new solutions that work for everyone—it won't just keep the peace, but will also make your life richer in every way.

You may also need a little extra encouragement to step out of your comfort zone. You like the stability of your routines and the security of your close relationships—and there's nothing wrong with that! But experiencing new places, situations, and people can teach you so much about the world and yourself, so try to embrace the occasional adventure.

Journaling Page

Think about your goals for 2025. Which of your Taurus gifts— tenacity, determination, steadiness, an eye for beauty—will you call on to help you achieve them? Which elements of the Taurus personality do you want to lean into this year?

The Year Ahead for Taurus

The Eclipses

If you want a high-level picture of the story of your year ahead, the eclipses are a great place to begin. These tend to mark pivotal moments—beginnings, endings, major turning points—and the more closely they connect with points in your birth chart, the more powerful their effects are likely to feel. The year 2025 has four eclipses total: lunar eclipses in Virgo and Pisces and solar eclipses in Aries and Virgo.

The first of these is the lunar eclipse in Virgo on March 14th. With the Moon in your solar fifth house, there's the possibility of romantic shake-ups, especially if you're single. You could finally realize that your crush is all wrong for you, or that someone you'd never considered in a romantic light is actually exactly *right*.

A solar eclipse in Aries arrives two weeks later on March 29th. This eclipse asks you to take seriously your emotional and spiritual needs—which are every bit as important as your physical needs—and commit to honoring them in the year ahead. You tend to be practical in your approach to life, but this is a chance to tend to a different side of yourself.

The year's second eclipse season begins with a lunar eclipse in Pisces on September 7th. This one will likely focus on your social life in some way: maybe you'll experience drama in a community you're part of, or maybe you'll find a new friend group that makes you feel loved for who you really are.

The 2025 eclipses close out with a solar eclipse in Virgo on September 21st. After the revelations of the spring's Virgo lunar eclipse, this is your chance to go forward with a fresh understanding of what you need, what makes you happy, and even how to add some much-needed romance to your life.

The Big Picture

After the eclipses, one of the best ways to learn about the big-picture story of your year is to look to the outer planets of Jupiter, Saturn, Uranus, Neptune, and Pluto. Because these planets move much more slowly through the zodiac than the inner planets of Sun, Moon, Mercury, Venus, and Mars, their effects can be longer-lasting, and they can shed light on the overall path your life will take this year.

One of the most important pieces of information for you, Taurus, is that unpredictable **Uranus** continues its transit through your Sun sign. Uranus, the planet of innovation, revolution, and change, entered Taurus in May 2018, and since it's in your solar first house, you've probably been feeling the effects on a more personal level than most. It's possible that Uranus has activated your inner rebel or made you uncharacteristically restless. (It's also possible that the universe has seemed to thrust chaos upon you, in spite of your wishes!)

When it comes to Uranus transits, the only sure thing is change. (May 17th in particular, when the Sun and Uranus align in Taurus, may bring big changes to your life!) You should get some relief from personal upheavals after Uranus dips into Gemini in July, but you aren't off the hook quite yet. It'll move back into Taurus on November 7th, before finally completing this Taurus cycle for good in April of 2026—but you'll have a chance to catch your breath and make a plan for the future.

The year 2025 begins with luck planet **Jupiter** in Gemini, where it'll be for about half the year. This is your solar second house of money, possessions, and personal finances: good news for you! This could mean financial windfalls, an unexpected raise, or scoring an amazing deal. The key to making the most of this energy is to put yourself out there! Professional networking is especially likely to bear fruit, but even simple socializing, making friends, and chatting with strangers could bring surprising good luck. When Jupiter moves into Cancer on June 9th, treating others with compassion and generosity is the best way to attract good luck: good deeds and kind words will be rewarded.

Saturn and **Neptune** are both still moving through Pisces and your solar eleventh house for much of this year, an indicator that community will play a big role in your year. With Neptune in this house, where it's been since 2011, it's possible that you've been idealizing social groups or communities you're part of. While Neptune is retrograde from July to December, you may lose the rose-colored glasses and see things for what they are. With Saturn in Pisces, there's a good chance that you've been dealing with feelings of loneliness, questioning your place in your social group, or wishing you had a stronger community around you. The key, as with all Saturn transits, is to remember that if you're dissatisfied with your life, *it's possible to make a change*. It might take some hard work—building genuine community takes time and effort!—but it's well within reach. Both planets pop into Aries for part of the year before returning to Pisces, an indication that this phase of your life will conclude, but not *quite* yet.

Finally, slow-moving **Pluto** is still in the middle of a yearslong transit through Aquarius that won't end until 2043. More than any of the other outer planets, Pluto's effects tend to be felt collectively more than personally. (The exception would be if it connects with a point in your natal chart.) While Pluto moves through idealistic and technology-minded Aquarius, expect movements for social justice around the world to pick up steam and AI to become even more of a hot topic.

Your Ruling Planet

As a Taurus, you're ruled by luxurious Venus, so Venus retrograde is a key event for you to watch this year. Venus stations retrograde in Aries on March 1st, moves backward into Pisces on March 27th, and then begins moving forward again on April 12th. Your love life might feel a little dull, unsatisfying, or confusing during this time: don't blame yourself, and know that any weird feelings are probably temporary. This is also not the best time for beautification projects. From painting your living room to dyeing your hair a new color, wait until Venus is back on track! Pay attention, too, to Venus's interactions with unpredictable Uranus, especially on July 4th and November 29th. Whenever these two planets interact, you can expect surprises, from relationship drama to financial windfalls to new love with someone totally unexpected. Since Uranus is spending most of 2025 in Taurus, you may experience the thrills of these transits and interactions more than most!

January

Three planets are already retrograde as 2025 begins: Mars, Jupiter, and Uranus. This means that, no matter how ambitious your resolutions for the new year, you'll be best served by taking things slow to start out. Both the Sun and Mercury move into Aquarius this month (the Sun on the 19th and Mercury on the 27th), encouraging you to think about what you want for your career in the year ahead. Start thinking now about how you'd like to grow—and what resources you might look to for support.

Moon Cycles

The first big lunar event of 2025 is a Full Moon in Cancer on January 13th. The Moon in Cancer always brings a healing influence, so this is a good Moon for putting old dramas to bed. It's a new year, and the past doesn't have to define you.

On the 29th, the New Moon in Aquarius is an excellent opportunity to turn over a new leaf in your professional life. Apply for an exciting new role, ask for more opportunities to grow, or start hatching a plan to change your career path entirely.

Power Days

The 8th is a good day for planning travel—and saying *yes* to adventures of all kinds. On the 13th, try stepping outside your comfort zone: risks are likely to bring rewards. Keep an open mind when meeting people on the 23rd, and you could meet someone who's going to be important in your life.

Days to Watch For

On the 3rd, boredom or stress could cause you to lash out: be careful not to say something you'll end up regretting! The 15th might be lonely: be proactive about making plans so you aren't stuck waiting for the phone to ring. On the 21st, watch out for arguments—especially with a spouse, partner, or best friend.

February

If January felt slow or frustrating, things are likely to get more exciting for you now. Venus enters bold, fiery Aries on the 4th. If you've been waiting to ask someone out (or simply talk to your crush), this could be the perfect time—especially since Venus retrograde begins next month. You'll probably feel your confidence (especially when it comes to decisions about money) return when Jupiter retrograde ends on the 4th, and your overall energy pick up when Mars retrograde ends on the 23rd.

Moon Cycles

On the 12th, a Full Moon in Leo will likely activate your sentimental side! Your love for your family (*including* chosen family) is in full bloom. It's never a bad time to tell people how you feel, but right now especially, don't be scared to open up.

Then on the 27th, new friendships (or romances that *start* as friendships) could begin under the New Moon in Pisces. The important thing right now is to be clear with yourself about what you really want—*before* things get serious—and not to settle for anything less.

Power Days

On the 7th, your charm and communication skills are unparalleled: you'll especially shine in negotiations or tricky conversations at work. The 19th is an ideal day to ask somebody out, especially if it's someone you've liked for a long time. On the 27th, your intuition is spot-on, so listen to it.

Days to Watch For

On the 5th, interpersonal conflicts you've been avoiding may finally boil over: make the effort to put things right again. On the 10th, your words may be misconstrued: especially in texts and emails, make sure you're saying what you really mean. On the 11th, *walk away* if you're getting upset: outbursts will only lead to trouble.

March

With two inner planet retrogrades (Venus retrograde begins on the 1st and Mercury on the 15th) plus two eclipses, March is one of the more action-packed months of 2025. All the excitement may disrupt your routines and cause some stress, but if you can keep an open mind and go with the flow, things might actually turn out *better* than you hoped. Mercury and Venus both spend time in your solar twelfth house, so meditation and deep personal reflection should be especially rewarding.

Moon Cycles

Under the lunar eclipse in Virgo on the 14th, your secret daydreams might become reality. This could feel stressful or more dramatic than you bargained for, but try not to worry: the universe isn't going to throw anything at you that you can't handle.

On the 29th, the solar eclipse in Aries is a moment when it's extra important to recharge and re-center. Life may feel particularly wild right now, but remember that you *don't* have to respond in haste. Your instincts are solid: you'll act when you're ready.

Power Days

On the 4th, take a friendship (or relationship) to a new level of trust and connection. The 14th is a perfect day to face your fears and try something new. The 28th is a good day for socializing and dating: just make sure that you're doing what *you* want, not getting dragged along with the crowd.

Days to Watch For

Look out for conflict at work on the 3rd, and try to choose your battles. On the 17th, relationships might feel off-balance; if your finances aren't split equitably, now is the time to remedy it. The 21st may amplify any feelings of guilt or low self-esteem: trust that it'll pass, and don't take it out on your friends.

April

April brings all kinds of welcome astrological news for you. First, Mercury retrograde ends on the 7th, and Venus retrograde ends on the 12th. Expect daily life, and especially interpersonal interactions, to get a *lot* smoother. After Venus stations direct, *no* planets are retrograde for the rest of the month, making this a perfect time to take huge strides toward your goals. Then the Sun enters Taurus on the 19th! Taurus season creates the conditions for you to be your best self and to truly focus on your feelings, needs, and path in life.

Moon Cycles

On the 12th, the Full Moon in Libra may illuminate the truth of your most important relationships, for better or worse. You might feel a strong urge now to fix or change your loved ones: resist it! Remember that you can only change yourself.

Then on the 27th, a New Moon in Taurus arrives to initiate a new phase in your life. If you sometimes neglect your emotional needs in favor of more practical affairs, this is a time to change that, and to treat your feelings like they genuinely matter.

Power Days

You're firing on all cylinders on the 1st, and your good energy is likely to attract new friends and opportunities. On the 8th, you're extra attractive to potential friends and partners, so try to put yourself out there. On the 15th, amazing things will happen when you ask your community to support you.

Days to Watch For

Avoid making impulsive decisions on the 12th—at least wait a couple of days. If family conflict flares up on the 20th, focus on de-escalating things rather than "winning" the fight. On the 23rd, clashing egos could cause problems at work: just do your best to stay calm, grounded, and out of the fray.

May

Taurus season continues into May! And on the 10th, Mercury joins the Sun in Taurus. This is a time for you to express yourself confidently and unapologetically and to show others your authentic self. Just as importantly, it's a time for you to think critically about what kind of life you really want and what kind of person you want to be. Your mind is at its clearest, so use it—especially before the Sun enters Gemini on the 20th and Mercury follows on the 25th.

Moon Cycles

On the 12th, a Full Moon in Scorpio brings emotions about your relationships to the surface. If there are problems you've been avoiding talking about, or if you're worried there's something going on that you don't know about, now is the time to dive deep, be honest, and find answers.

On the 26th, a New Moon in Gemini invites you to lean into your curiosity. New people, new places, new routines: the world is big, and by giving yourself time to explore it to the fullest, you're giving yourself a chance to grow and feel good about yourself.

Power Days

The 17th may bring unexpected good news—but don't sit around waiting for it, or you might end up missing out! On the 20th, work hard and stay disciplined and it'll pay off in a real way. You may experience amazing flashes of insight and inspiration on the 24th: trust your intuition!

Days to Watch For

The 10th is *not* a good day for serious conversations (especially about relationship problems), so wait a day or two if you can.

On the 12th, you could see an unpleasant side of a friend or colleague. Try to avoid getting drawn into conflict that doesn't involve you. You might be irritable on the 25th: find someone you can vent to!

June

Headline news for you this month is that love planet Venus moves into Taurus on the 6th! It'll stay here all month long, making this one of the best months of the year for you in the romance department. It's also a good time for you to think seriously about money—how you make it, how you save it, and most importantly, what you use it for. This month will likely present opportunities for all kinds of sweetness, pleasure, and fun. Make the most of them.

Moon Cycles

The Full Moon in Sagittarius on the 11th makes emotions and relationships feel extra intense. Simple conversations can lead to deep soul-searching; small interactions can make you question your whole life. This is a good day to release old baggage in order to start something new.

On the 25th, a New Moon in Cancer offers you a chance to reset your relationship with yourself. Set aside some time to do whatever makes you feel powerful, happy, or just most like *you*: rest, get a haircut, or call up your friend who's always ready with a pep talk.

Power Days

The 11th is one of the best days imaginable for asking someone out—or for taking yourself on a date. Connections made on the 21st have a good chance of turning into a relationship; and if you're in a relationship already, be sure to spend quality time together. On the 26th, let your quirky side show!

Days to Watch For

Jealousy could become a problem on the 9th, but open and honest communication will go a long way toward fixing things. On the 15th, a lack of attention to detail could lead to major mistakes. On the 28th, it may be hard to find motivation, so try to avoid scheduling anything too stressful today.

July

This month brings some major shifts. First, three planets station retrograde: Neptune on the 4th, Saturn on the 13th, and Mercury on the 18th. Mercury's likely to create the most noticeable effects in your life. As always, back up your files, double-check your work, and have a backup plan in case things go wrong. Venus leaves Taurus on the 4th. And, finally, Uranus leaves Taurus on the 7th and enters Gemini! It'll return to Taurus a bit later this year, but for now, breathe a sigh of relief as your life gets a bit less chaotic.

Moon Cycles

On the 10th, the Full Moon in Capricorn is a sign of changes in your professional life. Maybe you've reached a turning point, or maybe you've decided you need something more. This Moon is a reminder that you don't have to settle for a life that's unsatisfying.

On the 24th, a New Moon in Leo could indicate a new relationship or the start of an especially creative period of your life, but try to avoid rushing into anything or making huge commitments just yet. Take it slow, and trust that things will unfold in their own time.

Power Days

The 4th could bring unexpected money your way (or unexpected romance). The 6th is a perfect day for working through relationship problems and coming up with solid, workable solutions. On the 19th, be assertive! You'll be surprised what you can get because you asked.

Days to Watch For

Expect emotional outbursts (from yourself *and* others) on the 7th, and try not to take things too personally! On the 18th, working through painful emotions with loved ones or a therapist can be incredibly healing—but it won't be easy. You might feel lonely or misunderstood on the 31st, but know that it won't last forever.

August

On the 6th, Mars moves into Libra. While it's there, you might find that tact and persuasiveness serve you better than your usual straightforward approach. If conflict arises, trust that it's possible to find a solution that works for everyone. On the 11th, Mercury retrograde ends! If, during the retrograde period, you dreamed up big adventures or considered changing your whole life, now is when you can start to take steps forward. Likewise, if you've been struggling to have challenging conversations, the words might come more easily.

Moon Cycles

The Full Moon in Aquarius on the 9th indicates a moment of recognition. Your colleagues will see how hard you've been working, and your community will notice how much you've been doing behind the scenes. You might get more attention than you bargained for!

On the 23rd, the New Moon in Virgo invites you to look at your life honestly and commit to changing the things you don't like. More than ever, it's important to live out your values: don't expect yourself to be perfect, only to do the best you can.

Power Days

You're lucky in love on the 11th, and people are attracted to your good energy! The 15th is a powerful day for love of all kinds—not just romance, but friendship and family love, too. On the 29th, the more generous you are with others, the more lucky *you* will be, too.

Days to Watch For

On the 5th, small disagreements could turn into big problems, so try to address issues early on. On the 14th, your own biases and preferences could prevent you from seeing a situation clearly. On the 27th, you may second-guess a close relationship: don't jump to conclusions, but talk it over with someone you trust.

September

On the 1st, Saturn, which is currently retrograde, moves from Aries into Pisces, where it will remain until 2026. During this period, you'll find the greatest success by working collaboratively with others: don't chase personal acclaim at the expense of your friends and colleagues, because it won't work out! When Venus moves into Virgo on the 19th, don't overlook the small stuff: dealing with the details now will allow you to truly relax and enjoy yourself. The biggest news is that this is an eclipse month! More on that below.

Moon Cycles

The lunar eclipse in Pisces arrives on the 7th to supercharge your creativity and ambition. Let go of old dreams you've outgrown, and don't be held back by the past: let your imagination soar as you imagine the future you want to inhabit.

If you've been facing a tough decision—especially one related to romance or dating—the solar eclipse in Virgo on the 21st might force your hand. Chances are you know deep down what you want. Let this eclipse be the push you needed to finally make your choice.

Power Days

On the 11th, your creativity is flowing, and you can charm just about anyone you meet. The 13th is an ideal day for making plans, whether you're planning meetings or parties. On the 26th, don't be scared to ask for support when you need it: it could bring you closer to your loved ones.

Days to Watch For

If friends or colleagues seem to get in your way on the 20th, the best thing to do is just be patient. You may argue with loved ones (especially your partner, if you're in a relationship) on the 24th, but try to be kind and fair. On the 27th, it's easy to blow minor relationship conflicts *way* out of proportion.

October

On the 13th, Venus moves into Libra. Depending on what you're looking for, this can be a good time for going out and meeting new people, for planning romantic outings with your partner, or for showing *yourself* some extra care. The Sun enters Scorpio—and your solar seventh house of partnership and marriage—on the 22nd, so expect lots of activity in that area of your life! This could mean you'll meet your future partner, or it could mean you'll do a lot of learning about what you want and need from a relationship.

Moon Cycles

On the 6th, a Full Moon in Aries makes you *highly* sensitive to the people, energies, and emotions around you. You may be tempted to leap into action based on what you're feeling now, but try to wait a few days until the dust settles before you make any major moves.

On the 21st, a New Moon in Libra offers you the opportunity to think about what you really want to contribute to the world around you. Ask yourself what contributions you want to make in the days and weeks ahead, and how you want to support the people you love.

Power Days

On the 9th, opening up and letting others see your true, authentic self could lead to lasting love. On the 14th, you may meet someone intriguing who's *way* outside your normal "type." The 23rd gives you the strength and courage to stand up for yourself or the people you care about.

Days to Watch For

On the 8th, a bad mood could cause you to pick unnecessary fights: try to find somewhere positive to channel any cranky energy. You might be especially anxious or lonely on the 11th. Don't blame yourself; it's just one of those days. On the 17th, overconfidence could cause problems: don't promise what you can't deliver!

November

Another Mercury retrograde spans most of November (it begins on the 9th and ends on the 29th), so be extra careful to communicate clearly, and give others some grace if they get the words wrong). Especially since Mercury spends part of this retrograde in Sagittarius, it might be best to avoid travel if you can—or, if you're going ahead anyway, to spring for travel insurance and refundable tickets. Uranus moves back into Taurus on the 7th.

Expect for life to get a bit unpredictable again—or for your rebellious side to come out.

Moon Cycles

The Full Moon in Taurus happens on the 5th, and the more secure you feel—at work, in your relationships, or in life overall—the more you'll be able to let your authentic self shine. Whatever you've been building toward in life, you'll likely see signs of major progress now.

On the 20th, the New Moon in Scorpio is all about your close relationships. What's been getting in the way of genuine intimacy? If you've experienced barriers to real trust, this is your opportunity to start the work of overcoming them.

Power Days

The 6th is a good day for making commitments that you can stick to—whether to others or to yourself. Good luck comes your way on the 17th, and networking is likely to lead to great results. On the 20th, your intuition is especially sharp, so trust yourself (even if you can't explain *why* you feel the way you do).

Days to Watch For

On the 4th, watch out for self-sabotaging behaviors, and remember that you deserve happiness. Your mental energy might be scattered on the 19th: you can avoid big mistakes by being slow and deliberate and double-checking your work. On the 21st, plans are likely to be disrupted, so try to stay flexible.

December

Three planets move into Capricorn this month: Mars on the 15th, the Sun on the 21st, and Venus on the 24th. These combined planetary energies make this month (especially the second half of it) a good time for focusing on your long-term goals. Where do you want to be in a year, in five, in ten—not just in your career, but in your life? What is your broader purpose?

Moon Cycles

On the 4th, a Full Moon in Gemini activates big feelings about money, possessions, or your physical security. You could get great financial news—or you could find yourself getting *very* stressed about finances. Either way, the best thing to do now is learn, ask questions, and talk things over.

On the 19th, a New Moon in Sagittarius encourages you to take control of your life. While there's plenty out there that you can't control, this New Moon reminds you that you're way more powerful than you sometimes give yourself credit for. What changes can *you* make?

Power Days

On the 3rd, following your instincts will serve you better than even the most carefully laid plan. The 29th offers you a confidence boost: make the most of it and don't second-guess yourself! The 30th is a good day for taking a relationship to the next level.

Days to Watch For

On the 1st, someone close to you might make you feel bad about yourself (probably unintentionally). Speak up or things won't get better. On the 10th, think (and, more importantly, *listen*) before you speak! Don't follow wild impulses on the 13th—at least sleep on it first.

♊

Gemini

The Twins
May 21 to June 21

Element: Air
Ruling planet: Mercury
Keyword: Curiosity
Key phrase: I think

Gemstone: Tourmaline
Power stones: Ametrine, citrine, emerald
Color: Yellow
Flower: Lily of the valley

All about Gemini

Strengths and Gifts

Gemini is the last sign of springtime and the first air sign of the astrological year. It comes directly after stubborn, dependable Taurus—and in contrast, you, Gemini, are adaptable and open-minded. You're witty and sociable, and you love meeting new people, hearing new stories, and learning new things about the world.

One of your best traits is your curiosity. You approach the world with the spirit of a lifelong learner. You're full of fun facts and weird anecdotes about everything from natural history to comic books, from economics to knitting. Instead of diving deep into one topic, you like to know a little bit about everything.

While some people prefer for every day to be more or less the same, you thrive on variety. You'd rather sample everything on a restaurant's menu than order the same dish every time; you'd rather try a different perfume every day than settle on a signature scent. The world is full of interesting things to learn and experience, and you don't want to miss out on any of it!

Thanks to this open-mindedness and eagerness to learn, you can get along with virtually anyone. You approach people with an open heart and a genuine interest in learning about them, which means you make friends quickly and easily. You're probably the type of person who can strike up a conversation anywhere—from a fancy dinner to the line at the grocery store—and enjoy the interaction.

You're excellent at picking up on social vibes and can adapt easily to new situations and settings. New job, new city, new friend group? No problem: you know how to seamlessly fit right in. You can be equally comfortable in a boardroom and a dive bar; just as comfortable at a punk show as you are at the opera. Wherever you go, you know how to fit in, find your people, and look like you've been there your whole life.

Gemini is ruled by Mercury, the planet of thought, language, and communication, which means that you're observant and *smart*. Your mind is constantly working, brimming with questions, stories, and ideas. You're fascinated by all that the world has to offer, and this makes *you* a fascinating person in turn—interesting, fun, even a little dazzling to be around.

Friendship and Love

With your quick wit and natural charm, you're an excellent date. Not only can you tell a great story, but you're also good at asking other people questions about themselves (and, more importantly, you're genuinely interested in what they have to say!). Whether you're meeting up for a casual coffee or an elegant dinner, you can make just about any occasion fun, for you *and* for the other person. If you do experience dating troubles, the problem probably isn't capturing other people's attention—it's finding someone who can keep *yours*!

While the physical connection matters to you (of course!), being on the same wavelength mentally is ultimately much more attractive. You could meet the most beautiful person in the universe, but if they can't tell a joke or don't have anything interesting to say, forget it! You want a partner who can match your banter and keep you on your toes. You're probably most drawn to people who are funny, who have interesting hobbies and interests of their own, or who can challenge you intellectually. For you, one of the absolute most important criteria in a relationship is that you aren't bored.

The term "social butterfly" was probably invented to describe a Gemini! When it comes to friendship, you probably have lots of good pals in lots of different social circles. While you certainly have close relationships, you're not the type to cling to the same bestie you've had since kindergarten without ever branching out—you like to share your love and attention with as many people as you can.

This means that sometimes others may find you somewhat difficult to get close to. They want your undivided attention when you want to be out exploring the world! This doesn't mean you're not loyal—when you commit, you *really* commit—it just means your partner needs to understand that they shouldn't try to curtail your freedom. For your part, it means that you might need to be extra intentional about giving the people closest to you the care and attention they need.

Work and Money

Because your mind is so active, you tend to struggle in jobs that are repetitive or boring. You need mental stimulation! This means that you probably thrive in jobs where you're able to put your intellect to work (especially jobs that involve writing and communication) or where you get to interact with lots of different types of people. You might not think of yourself as a particularly ambitious person—you aren't necessarily motivated by wealth or public recognition—but it's important to keep seeking out challenges at work, if only so that you don't get bored!

When it comes to money, you're often a little scattered. When your checking account is full, it's easy for you to drop *lots* of money on new hobbies that you end up losing interest in, or on breathtaking outfits you wear only once. You may have big financial goals, but you aren't always the most disciplined in working toward them. Following a budget is a lot less fun than winging it, but it could help you bring some order to your finances.

Struggles and Growth

Your curiosity is one of the best things about you. It helps you learn about the world and keep an open mind about people, and it makes you a truly engaging person to spend time with. It can also, though, make you easily distracted. When you're constantly learning new skills, you risk never getting really good at any one of them. If you're always thinking up new projects, you risk never finishing any of the ones you've already started. If you can learn to balance your natural curiosity with a bit of focus and discipline, you can achieve great things.

Similarly, your interest in meeting new people can sometimes get in the way of building true intimacy with the friends you already have. In part, this is because intimacy can be a little scary for you! You tend to prefer to keep things light and fun, rather than diving into more complicated emotions. Getting serious in friendships and in love requires some courage, but ultimately it's worth it.

Journaling Page

Think about your goals for 2025. Which of your Gemini gifts—curiosity, sociability, adaptability, sense of humor—will you call on to help you achieve them? Which elements of the Gemini personality do you want to lean into this year?

The Year Ahead for Gemini

The Eclipses

Eclipses—when the Earth, Moon, and Sun are perfectly aligned—happen every year, and are strong indicators about the overall story of a year. They offer us clues to questions like: What is beginning and what is ending? What major pivots or unexpected turning points are on the horizon? This year has four eclipses total: two lunar eclipses (in Virgo and Pisces) and two solar eclipses (in Aries and Virgo).

The first eclipse season of 2025 arrives in March, with a lunar eclipse in Virgo on the 14th. Some long-simmering family drama might finally be dealt with in the open, or you might be inspired to take on a big home improvement project. If your home or family situation hasn't felt right, this is a major opportunity to make it better.

Then on March 29th, a solar eclipse in Aries inspires you to reconnect with a community you've lost touch with—or to find a new community where you'll be welcomed for your *whole* self. You shouldn't have to hide or suppress parts of who you are in order to feel a sense of belonging.

The second eclipse season of 2025 takes place in September, beginning with a lunar eclipse in Pisces on the 7th. This is a chance for you to see how your career fits in with your deeper purpose in life. (And if it *doesn't* fit in, or you don't like what you see, it's a perfect opportunity to make some necessary changes.)

Then on September 21st, a solar eclipse in Virgo is a chance to rewrite your story with your family (or chosen family). It isn't too late to make amends, to change dynamics that aren't working for you, to share your perspective openly, to let your loved ones know what you need from them. Things won't become perfect overnight, but they genuinely can get better.

The Big Picture

While the eclipses tell a very personal story about your year to come, it's also useful to look to the outer planets of Jupiter, Saturn, Uranus, Neptune, and Pluto. While the inner planets (Sun, Moon, Mercury, Venus, and Mars) can be used for tracking moods and day-to-day occurrences, the distant, slow-moving outer planets offer us a broader look at the forces at work throughout 2025.

Lucky you, Gemini: **Jupiter**, planet of growth, abundance, and good fortune, spends nearly half the year in your sign, until it moves into Cancer on June 9th. This is the continuation of a story that began in May of 2024, when Jupiter first entered Gemini, and should be a lucky time for you. Success comes more easily to you now, your talents shine, and other people are, quite simply, charmed by you! During this period, you'll probably feel some extra self-confidence: make the most of it by taking risks, starting new ventures, and applying for opportunities that will truly challenge you and help you grow. (June 8th, when Mercury and Jupiter align, is an especially good day for making bold plans for the future.) Overall, do your best not to stay in your comfort zone while Jupiter is in Gemini, but instead stretch yourself, take risks, and broaden your horizons.

Unpredictable **Uranus** will also spend part of 2025 in Gemini, promising excitement and change. Uranus enters Gemini on July 7th, stations retrograde on September 6th, and finally leaves your sign to move back into Taurus on November 7th. (In 2026, Uranus will enter your sign for a much longer time—think of this period in 2025 as a prelude.) During these months, the best thing you can do is open your mind and heart to change—even if it's change that you weren't expecting or didn't ask for. The ups and downs you experience now will make you happier, and more free, in the long run.

Saturn, planet of discipline and limitations, spends much of this year in Pisces and your solar tenth house of career, achievement, and reputation. This means that 2025 could be a big career year for you. If you've been laying the groundwork and working hard toward a goal, chances are good that you'll see results this year. **Neptune**, planet of dreams and fantasy, also begins the year in Pisces. No matter how much success Saturn brings, Neptune's influence may cause you to question the deeper purpose of the work you do: Are you on the right path? Does your work fulfill you on a level beyond just the money? Listen to your heart, and don't be afraid to make a change. Both Saturn and Neptune will also spend some time in Aries this year: Saturn from May 24th until it returns to Pisces on September 1st, and Neptune from March 30th until it returns to Pisces on October 22nd. While both planets spend time in Aries, expect a fresh dose of self-confidence—but also a reminder of your bigger ideals and your responsibilities to your community.

Finally, **Pluto**—the most distant and slowest-moving of all the planets—is still making its way through Aquarius, a transit that will last until 2043. Even more than the rest of the outer planets, Pluto's effects tend to be felt on a societal, not personal, level, except for when it connects to important points in your own chart. Pluto's movement through Aquarius may influence you to get involved with a social movement, and it will certainly be an opportunity for you to learn a lot about the world around you.

Your Ruling Planet

As a Gemini, you're ruled by bright and quick-witted Mercury, so you'll want to pay particular attention to Mercury retrogrades. There are three this year: March 15th to April 7th, July 18th to August 11th, and November 9th to November 29th. There can be a lot of fear-mongering out there about Mercury retrograde—

but you don't need to be scared! To be sure, Mercury retrograde can sometimes coincide with tech glitches and travel delays (the November retrograde is particularly likely to cause travel snags), and it can make communication a little less smooth. As much as possible, try to avoid scheduling important events during these times, and try to extend a little grace—to others *and* yourself—when miscommunications inevitably arise. More importantly, Mercury retrograde is an amazing time for reflection. If you're the type of person who likes to always be on the go, the best thing you can do is *slow down* when Mercury is retrograde. You might come to big insights about yourself and your relationships if you use this time to reflect.

January

As 2025 begins, three planets are already retrograde: Mars, Jupiter, and Uranus. The planets are making everything move a *lot* more slowly than you'd like, so don't get discouraged if your big ideas for the new year don't take off just yet. With the Sun beginning the year in Capricorn, and Mercury joining it on the 8th, you might be feeling uncharacteristically serious, even a little down on yourself—but when both planets enter Aquarius (the Sun on the 19th and Mercury on the 27th), expect to feel a lot more optimistic.

Moon Cycles

The first Full Moon of the year, in Cancer, arrives on January 13th. If there's a financial situation that's been stressing you out, this Moon could be your opportunity to fix things—whether by making a budget, having a serious money talk, or even receiving an unexpected windfall.

On the 29th, the New Moon in Aquarius asks you to dream big. This Moon is here to remind you that you don't have to do things the way you've always done them. Experiment! Travel the world! Your future is calling, so lean into the excitement.

Power Days

Luck is on your side on the 10th—and the more you share your good fortune, the luckier you'll get. The 12th is an ideal day to ask for a big favor or a raise. If you've been thinking about starting a new project or booking an international trip, go for it on the 30th.

Days to Watch For

Don't get cocky on the 4th! A little humility right now will prevent all kinds of headaches later on. Avoid impulse purchases on the 14th: it's *very* easy to overspend on stuff you don't need (or even really want!). Your judgment could be a little blurred on the 16th, so get some advice before making any important decisions.

February

When Jupiter retrograde ends on the 4th, expect to start feeling lucky, optimistic, and confident. Everything, from work to relationships, should seem just a little easier now. Mars retrograde also ends on the 23rd, offering you a further confidence boost. When the Sun and Mercury both move into Pisces (Mercury on the 14th, the Sun on the 18th), your intuition gets stronger. Trust your gut (especially when it comes to work drama), and don't be scared to make a change—whether that's asking for a raise, taking classes, or looking for a new job.

Moon Cycles

On the 12th, a Full Moon in Leo could stir up emotional interactions with friends, neighbors, or even casual acquaintances. Things could get a little dramatic, but that's not such a bad thing! Open, honest communication will solve problems and open doors.

Then on the 27th, the New Moon in Pisces could find you feeling a bit stressed and emotional at work. You'll probably be extra sensitive to criticism—but there are people around you who truly want to support you, so don't close yourself off.

Power Days

Good news may come your way on the 3rd! If you've been involved in lengthy negotiations of any kind, they may finally wrap up in your favor. The 6th is a great day for dating and socializing: you can charm just about anyone. On the 16th, honest conversations about your feelings can lead to deeper intimacy and genuine love.

Days to Watch For

Avoid making commitments or grand gestures on the 13th: you'll probably end up wishing you had waited! On the 20th, it's easy to make promises (especially at work) that you won't be able to deliver on, so make an extra effort to be realistic about what you can do. On the 27th, your impulses may be unreliable: trust your rational side.

March

The eclipses are the most important cosmic events to watch for this month (more on that below), but Mercury and Venus retrograde also begin this month. Venus stations retrograde in Aries on the 1st, and dating and romance are likely to get more difficult. In particular, trying to turn a friendship into a romance during this time will likely lead to unforeseen complications (but it isn't impossible!). Mercury retrograde starts on the 15th and could lead to drama or misunderstandings within your friend group, but it won't be anything that patience and communication can't fix.

Moon Cycles

The year's first eclipse—a lunar eclipse in Virgo—arrives on the 14th. It could prompt a major epiphany about love, family, or your sense of home. Like all eclipses, it could be stressful in the moment, but ultimately it'll empower you to make some changes you've needed for a long time.

Then on the 29th, the solar eclipse in Aries is all about meeting new people and forging deeper relationships with people you've known for a long time. Chance encounters and random conversations (especially about your emotions) could lead to lifelong friendships.

Power Days

A soulmate or best friend could enter your life on the 5th: if it feels like destiny, it probably is! You attract success and generosity on the 15th: this is a good day to apply for new opportunities, share your work, and get your name out there. If you experience a flash of inspiration on the 25th, listen to it.

Days to Watch For

You may feel stretched too thin on the 2nd, especially at work. Make a plan and prioritize! If you've let relationship tensions go unaddressed, they'll rise to the surface on the 6th. On the 20th, it feels like everyone is in your business. Make a point of setting the boundaries you need.

April

The retrogrades that began last month both end in April: Mercury stations direct on the 7th, and Venus on the 12th. With no planets retrograde for the rest of the month *and* lucky Jupiter still in your sign, this is a phenomenal time for making moves and carrying out plans. When the Sun enters Taurus on the 19th, it's a good time to reflect on your habits and routines. Are they supporting you or holding you back? Even if you aren't ready to discuss it with anyone else, at least be honest with yourself.

Moon Cycles

If you've been dreaming about a crush, there's a good chance that things will blossom into something more under the Full Moon in Libra on the 12th. Or, if you've been working on a creative project, you're likely to make a major breakthrough.

On the 27th, a New Moon in Taurus encourages you to take time for yourself, away from the distractions of your social life. When you're alone with yourself, what do you really want? What makes you feel fulfilled? Listen to the insights that come to you today.

Power Days

The 2nd is a strong day for new beginnings and a great chance to start a project or join a club or social group. The 6th is an all-around lucky day. You'll feel like other people (and the universe!) have your back, so make the most of it. On the 29th, don't wait for others to make things happen: take the lead.

Days to Watch For

Work and relationships feel just a little *off* on the 3rd: trust that it isn't your fault and will blow over soon. It's tempting to settle for less than you deserve on the 9th: don't do it! On the 17th, it may feel like your friends or partner are taking you for granted: tell them how you feel.

May

This is an absolutely stellar month for you, Gemini. Not only is lucky Jupiter still in your corner, but the Sun enters Gemini on the 20th, followed by your ruling planet, Mercury, on the 25th, followed by a supportive New Moon in Gemini on the 26th. With all these planets piling up in your sign, it's like some of the barriers to your happiness fall away. Luck is on your side, and it's easier to be your authentic self. Things are likely to turn out in your favor this month, so don't hold back!

Moon Cycles

You might be incredibly hard on yourself—and friends and family—under the Full Moon in Scorpio on the 12th. If you have criticisms to make, try to be honest but kind. Remind yourself that you don't actually need to be perfect to deserve love.

On the 26th, the New Moon in Gemini is a time for tuning in to *yourself*—your needs, desires, moods—and letting them guide you. Sometimes you put everyone else's needs above your own. This Moon is your chance to remember that *you* matter, too.

Power Days

Conversations with others (friends, partners, even your thera-pist) on the 18th can lead to fresh perspectives, new confidence, and a lot more compassion for yourself. The 22nd is an ideal day for setting goals and dreaming *big* about your future: don't hold back. The 26th is one of the best astrological days all year for you: projects started today are likely to lead to huge success.

Days to Watch For

Expect to be extra moody on the 7th: avoid making binding com-mitments today, because you'll probably feel differently tomor-row. It's easy to take wrong turns or get lost down rabbit holes on the 12th: ask for directions when you need to. The 15th may see you falling back into bad habits or harmful relationship dynamics if you aren't careful.

June

The big event of June, for you, is that Jupiter leaves Gemini and enters Cancer on the 9th. (Mercury and the Sun both move into Cancer, too, on the 8th and 20th, respectively.) While you may feel a bit less personally charmed, this isn't a bad thing! Over the course of the next year, Jupiter in Cancer is likely to bring finan-cial good fortune your way with a surprising windfall, a raise, or a lucky investment. Maximize your luck by investing in your relationships and being generous with those you love, especially family.

Moon Cycles

On the 11th, the Full Moon in Sagittarius is a day to focus on your closest relationships. Existing relationships might progress to the next level today; if you're looking for love, you could meet someone special. No matter what happens, the key is to be honest about how you're feeling!

Under the New Moon in Cancer on the 25th, it's easy to imagine that money will solve all your problems—but it isn't necessarily true! Don't be fooled by get-rich-quick schemes (no matter *how* tempting they appear). Right now, focus on investing in your relationships instead.

Power Days

The 4th is an extra romantic day for you. If you're looking to meet someone, attending a social gathering will probably work much better than any dating app! You'll get an extra burst of energy on the 5th—use it to tackle the toughest items on your to-do list. Ongoing conflicts are likely to resolve favorably on the 8th.

Days to Watch For

Arguments with a family member are likely on the 2nd: take the time to hear them out. On the 3rd, your head and your heart could clash: get advice from others, but remember that ultimately it's *your* life. Work (or your coworkers) may be annoying on the 18th, but things probably aren't as bad as they seem to you.

July

Venus moves into Gemini on the 4th, which is great news for your love life—and your social life in general. While Venus is in your sign, it's easy to let your charm shine through, and you'll find that people are naturally drawn to you. (Venus only stays here until the 30th, so make a point of socializing and enjoying yourself now!) Even bigger news is that unpredictable Uranus moves into Gemini as well on the 7th. Between now and November, when Uranus returns to Taurus, be prepared for surprises.

Moon Cycles

On the 10th, the Full Moon in Capricorn might stir up *strong* emotions. Pay extra close attention to any personal or professional jealousy that arises. Could it be pointing you toward big dreams or deep desires you haven't yet acknowledged, even to yourself?

On the 24th, a New Moon in Leo is an opportunity to change your mind about something (or someone) important in your life. Acknowledge that first impressions aren't always correct, and trust that a fresh mindset will create fresh opportunities for you.

Power Days

If you're clear and honest about your relationship expectations on the 6th, there's a good chance you'll get exactly what you need. Intense romantic encounters are possible on the 7th: dive in headfirst! Don't overthink things on the 20th! If you trust your instincts, you'll probably end up somewhere magical.

Days to Watch For

Impulsive behavior could get you into trouble on the 13th: stick to your usual routine for now, even if it seems boring. On the 23rd, it's easy to fall fast and hard for somebody totally wrong for you. Take it slow and don't lose your head! Don't jump to conclusions on the 26th: your first impression may not be the right one.

August

On the 6th, Mars moves into Libra, where it'll stay until late September. While it's here, try to avoid getting drawn into conflict: compromise will serve you much better than outright competition. Mercury retrograde ends on the 11th! When your ruling planet begins moving forward again, it's like any fog in your mind finally lifts. You'll be filled with ideas, and you'll want to share them with people. You'll really shine in big group settings, and this is a great time to speak your mind and engage in friendly debate.

Moon Cycles

The Aquarius Full Moon on the 9th is all about experimentation, especially if you've felt bored lately. Do something you wouldn't normally, like taking a new route to work, going to the movies on a whim, or giving a chance to someone who isn't your normal type.

On the 23rd, under the New Moon in Virgo, alone time is crucial. Don't pack your schedule with work or social events— you need time to breathe and to think today. Even if you can only get ten minutes to yourself, take those ten minutes!

Power Days

On the 8th, you'll have the courage to break free from whatever is holding you back, whether unsupportive relationships or negative beliefs about yourself. On the 11th, you can make bold changes *without* messing up the good things in your life. The 26th brings exciting social encounters that help you see the world (or yourself!) in a new way.

Days to Watch For

It's easy to overreact to minor problems on the 3rd: don't let small things ruin good relationships! Sudden changes you make on the 10th probably won't turn out the way you hoped, so try to wait a few days before making a big move. Unexpected changes might mess up your plans on the 24th: be prepared to be flexible.

September

Saturn, which only changes signs roughly every 2.5 years, moves into Pisces on the 1st. This is a big change—and likely a positive one for you! While Saturn transits always come with their challenges, you're likely to see your hard work pay off during this time. Promotions, exciting new responsibilities, or public recognition of your work are all likely during this period—especially if you've been putting in the effort. Uranus stations retrograde in Gemini on the 6th; while you're still likely to feel the unpredictable effects of Uranus, they should be less disruptive.

Moon Cycles

On the 7th, the lunar eclipse in Pisces shines a spotlight on you! For better or worse, everyone is paying attention to you. Especially if you've been working extra hard this year, this eclipse could reward you with a life-changing amount of public recognition.

Then on the 21st, the solar eclipse in Virgo supports you in noticing what isn't right about your surroundings and making a plan to fix it. You might begin dreaming about moving, especially to be closer to family or other loved ones.

Power Days

You don't have to do what anyone else expects of you: if you've been considering a big life change that might surprise your loved ones, the 4th is your chance to go for it. You could get exciting news, like an award or a promotion, on the 18th. Open-mindedness will be rewarded in a big way on the 23rd.

Days to Watch For

Miscommunications are likely on the 3rd, so if something seems *off*, be sure to ask for clarification or more information. On the 14th, expect a little extra tension in almost all areas of your life, and try to be patient. If you've been feeling smothered by other people's expectations, you may lash out on the 20th.

October

Venus enters its home sign of Libra on the 13th, making the second half of this month an excellent time to focus on romance, beauty, and whatever makes you happy. For you especially, Venus in Libra is a time of fun! Try not to schedule any major work events during this time, because your motivation will probably dip. On the 29th, Mercury moves into Sagittarius (and your solar seventh house of partnership). Use this time to get completely honest with your partner, plan an adventure with your best friend, or negotiate a new contract.

Moon Cycles

On the 6th, the Full Moon in Aries shows you the importance of community. The more care you've put into your friendships, the more people will come through for you today—whether you're looking for fun and adventure or some emotional support.

The New Moon in Libra on the 21st is likely one of the most creatively rich days of the year for you. And if you meet someone new (or run into an old flame) under this Moon, chances are good that it will lead to a deep connection—maybe even love.

Power Days

It might be *very* hard to focus on your responsibilities on the 4th, so be extra careful not to let anything important fall through the cracks. On the 9th, it's easy to fall for people or opportunities that are too good to be true: do your due diligence! A meet-cute or financial windfall may come your way on the 14th.

Days to Watch For

On the 7th, you may feel an urgent pressure to change your life (or yourself), but you'll get better results if you take your time. You may feel lonely and misunderstood on the 11th, but the feeling should pass soon. On the 29th, think before you speak, or you could end up saying something you regret.

November

The final Mercury retrograde of the year spans most of this month, beginning on the 9th and ending on the 29th. You might accidentally hurt your loved ones' feelings. Don't be scared to apologize, and things should blow over quickly. Mars moves into Sagittarius on the 4th, setting the scene for conflict—but also real growth—in intimate relationships. You'll be rewarded when Venus moves into Sagittarius on the 30th: this is one of the best times possible for starting new relationships, mending frayed friendships, and generally getting the love you need.

Moon Cycles

The Full Moon in Taurus on the 5th may highlight your insecurities, but it also offers you an amazing opportunity to work through them. Take care of your physical self by eating well and resting, and make a point of sharing your feelings with someone you trust.

On the 20th, the New Moon in Scorpio is an ideal time to set fresh intentions about your health. Whether you need to get on a regular sleep schedule, exercise more, or just make that dentist appointment you've been putting off, this is your time to commit to it.

Power Days

On the 3rd, put your energy toward helping others. It's the right thing to do, and it could also bolster *your* reputation. The 12th is an excellent day to defend your boundaries and stand up for yourself: just be careful not to create unnecessary conflict. The 17th brings big opportunities for wealth and success, so make the most of them.

Days to Watch For

You could be blindsided by sudden conflict on the 4th: expect some disruption to your routines, and try to keep a cool head. You could have big doubts about your relationship on the 6th, but they'll most likely blow over quickly. The 7th probably isn't a great day for socializing—better to lie low and take care of yourself.

December

The Full and New Moons should be especially sweet to you this month—more on that below. Other than that, this month is heavy on Capricorn energy, with Mars, the Sun, and Venus all entering the most serious of the signs (on the 15th, 21st, and 24th, respectively). If you're like most Geminis, you probably like to keep things light and breezy, but this month, try to approach your life, work, and relationships with a little more seriousness. Trust that hard work, in all areas of your life, will be rewarded.

Moon Cycles

On the 4th, a Full Moon in Gemini shows you just how much you've grown over the past year, and you could hit a big personal milestone. Give yourself a pat on the back, and think about how you can give back to the people who helped you.

If you've been hoping to take a relationship to a new level of intimacy, the Sagittarius New Moon on the 19th is a great time to make your move. Or, if you've been struggling in an existing relationship, this is an opportunity for a reset.

Power Days

Any love relationships, from crushes to marriages, could become deeper and more passionate on the 2nd. If you aren't in a relationship, the 19th is one of the best days possible for starting one. Being vulnerable and opening up about your feelings on 26th will lead to emotional strength and stronger relationships.

Days to Watch For

As much as possible, avoid tough conversations or negotiations on the 8th: things are unlikely to go your way just now. You'll probably be under a lot of pressure at work on the 16th, and your confidence may take a hit on the 20th—but in both situations, with a bit of discipline and determination, you'll pull through just fine.

Cancer

The Crab
June 21 to July 22

Element: Water
Ruling planet: Moon
Keyword: Nurturing
Key phrase: I feel

Gemstone: Pearl
Power stones: Moonstone, chrysocolla
Color: Silver
Flower: Larkspur

All about Cancer

Strengths and Gifts

Cancer, the crab, is the first sign of summer and the first water sign of the astrological year. Like all the water signs, you experience the world first and foremost on an emotional level. You're perceptive, intuitive, and in touch with your feelings. While Gemini, the sign that comes immediately before yours in the zodiac, may prefer to keep things on the surface level, you tend to feel everything *deeply*.

This depth is one of the most striking things about you. Nothing about you, Cancer, is shallow or simplistic! You think deeply, feel deeply, and experience your relationships on a profound level. Others often find you intriguing (sometimes even a little mysterious!) for this reason. Like your symbol, the crab, you have a protective outer shell, and it can take some work to get to know the "real" you. You're not likely to share your deepest emotions or your full life story the very first time you meet someone new, but it's clear upon first impression that you're a fascinating person with hidden depths.

Because you're willing to dive deep into the world of emotions, you're more intuitive than most people. You're excellent at listening to your gut—and you probably know from experience that it won't lead you astray, even when it's not exactly logical. Even more than that, you're good at reading other people's emotions and picking up on subtext. You don't need everything to be spelled out for you: your friends or your partner may try to hide their true feelings, but you're sensitive enough to pick up on what's really going on.

This sensitivity to emotions—your own *and* others'—means that you're a truly caring partner, family member, and friend. You understand that feelings and relationships can be fragile things, and it's important to you to treat them with the care they deserve. You're good at nurturing others. From lending a sympathetic ear, to calling to check in when you know a friend's been feeling down, to sending flowers on birthdays, you understand that the small stuff matters.

Because of your caring nature, others sometimes underestimate you, seeing kindness as a sign of weakness. This couldn't be further from the truth! You possess an unbreakable inner toughness. Especially when it comes to the people you love, you'll do just about anything to defend and take care of them.

Friendship and Love

Cancer is ruled by the Moon, the astrological planet of emotion. This means that you're right at home in the world of relationships, comfortable navigating all the complexities of love. You're generous and sensitive to others' needs, and your emotions run deep: *anyone*, friend or partner, should consider themselves lucky to be loved by you.

Your perceptiveness and sensitivity make you excellent at figuring out what other people need—but you don't always stop to think about what *you* need from relationships. If you're like most Cancers, security is incredibly important to you. While you're almost always up for an adventure, you want to know that you have a safe, peaceful home to return to at the end of the day. This applies equally to relationships: while it can be fun to run with the wild crowd, you're ultimately more drawn to people you can trust will make your life *less* chaotic, not more!

This doesn't mean you're quick to settle down—on the contrary, it can take you a surprisingly long time to open up, trust others, and commit. No matter how friendly and outgoing you may be, you probably keep new people—dates and friends alike—at arm's length. You take relationships seriously and hesitate to let anyone into your heart until you're sure they deserve it. This means that people who are trying to pursue a relationship with you can sometimes find you to be a tough nut to crack! Letting others in on your feelings doesn't always come naturally to you, but try to remember that when you *do* open up to the people you trust, it builds intimacy and strengthens your bond.

Even if you've managed to build up a tough exterior, underneath you're probably a deeply sensitive person. This is part of what makes you so lovely to be around—but it can also make you a bit touchy, easily wounded by thoughtless comments or actions. The key isn't to try, somehow, to make yourself less sensitive—that never works!—or to internalize your hurt feelings and let the problem fester, but to *tell people* how you're feeling.

Work and Money

Just as security is important to you in relationships, it's important in your work life, too. You probably aren't particularly motivated by money, acclaim, or the promise of climbing the corporate ladder. You work so that you can maintain a happy, peaceful life outside of work. While some people like to work in high risk, high reward environments, that's probably not for you. You'd prefer a steady paycheck and reasonable work-life balance. It's a classic stereotype that Cancers are well suited for work in the so-called caring professions, but the truth is that you're just as well suited for *any* work that involves developing relationships with others, from counseling to sales.

For you, money is important because of the security it provides. For this reason, you're probably pretty good at budgeting and saving. Knowing you've got some money stashed away for a rainy day is way more satisfying than the momentary thrill of a new purchase. Honestly, you probably deserve to treat yourself a little more! When you're making your budget, be sure to include a line for small luxuries, new clothes, or a beach vacation (Cancers thrive near the water!).

Struggles and Growth

Your sensitive nature and intuition serve you well in life. They make you amazing at reading the room, connecting with people, and caring for the people in your life. On the flip side, though, your sensitivity can mean that you take things too personally, read too much into other people's comments, or try to avoid conflict. The trouble is that some conflict is inevitable (and healthy conflict generally leads to stronger relationships and personal growth). For you, the challenge is to be brave, lean into uncomfortable conversations, and express your needs. It may be scary to put yourself out there, but you'll be glad you did.

Because of your caring nature, it's also sometimes hard for you to take your own needs and desires seriously. You have a tendency to put everyone else's well-being above your own—but that only ends up causing resentment. Practice advocating for yourself! And if you need to, remind yourself that this isn't selfishness. After all, there's no way to care for others if *your* cup is empty.

Journaling Page

Think about your goals for 2025. Which of your Cancer gifts—intuition, compassion, perceptiveness, capacity for love—will you call on to help you achieve them? Which elements of the Cancer personality do you want to lean into this year?

The Year Ahead for Cancer

The Eclipses

Some of the most important astrological dates to keep in mind for 2025 are the eclipses. Most years have about four of them, and by paying attention to them, you can track the pivotal moments and major dramas of the year. Some eclipses will affect you in big, life-changing ways, and others you'll feel more subtly—it depends on your personal birth chart. The year 2025 has four eclipses: lunar eclipses in Virgo and Pisces and solar eclipses in Aries and Virgo.

The first of these—the lunar eclipse in Virgo—arrives on March 14th. This is an excellent time for communication, especially about issues that have been nagging at you for a long time. It's much better to bring things out in the open than to let them continue to simmer! Under this eclipse, your words are *incredibly* powerful, so use them with intention and care.

Two weeks later, a solar eclipse in fiery Aries arrives on March 29th. This eclipse asks you to think about whether you're happy in your career—and if not, it invites you to think about what needs to change. If you're hesitant to make necessary changes, the universe just might give you an extra push, so don't be shy: follow your dreams and don't settle for less.

The second eclipse season of 2025 arrives in September, starting with a lunar eclipse in Pisces on the 7th. You're likely to feel incredibly restless right now, hungry for deeper meaning in your life. This could be an excellent time to go on a big solo trip: you'll learn *so* much about yourself.

Finally, the solar eclipse in Virgo on September 21st closes out this year's eclipses. If March's lunar eclipse in Virgo brought conflict or disagreements to the surface, this eclipse gives you a chance to move forward with a clear head and a clean slate.

The Big Picture

Okay, so you're ready for the eclipses. What else is coming in 2025? The next place to learn about the overall picture of the coming year is the outer planets: Jupiter, Saturn, Uranus, Neptune, and Pluto. The transits of these planets, which move slowly through the zodiac, can define months or even years (or longer!) of our lives, so it's wise to take a look at them when you're planning for the year ahead.

For you, Cancer, 2025 holds excellent news: lucky **Jupiter** moves into your Sun sign midway through the year! While Jupiter starts the year in Gemini, it moves into Cancer on June 9th, and will stay there through the rest of the year. During this time, it's like Jupiter is giving you an extra boost: work should go a little more smoothly, relationships should feel a bit more sparkly and special, and you can just be happy to be *you*. (This isn't to say that everything will be totally perfect, but even the bad days won't be quite so bad.) This whole period should be lovely, but a couple dates are *extra* noteworthy. On June 24th, the Sun and Jupiter align in Cancer. This is a very lucky day for beginning new projects, signing up for classes, or embarking on any journey that will expand your horizons. On August 12th, Venus and Jupiter align in Cancer. This is one of the best days possible for relationships. If you're already in one, spend quality time together today! If you're single, don't be surprised if you end up meeting somebody special. A word to the wise: while Jupiter transits are usually totally lovely, the one thing to watch out for is overconfidence! Try to stay humble, and don't take anything (or anyone!) for granted.

Saturn, planet of discipline and limitations, and **Neptune**, planet of dreams, both begin the year in Pisces, move into Aries midway through the year, then station retrograde and return to Pisces before 2025 is over. For you, Cancer, pay particular attention to the portion of this year when Saturn is in Aries, from May 24th to September 1st. This is likely to be the most professionally rewarding time of the year. That doesn't mean you need to work extra hard over the summer—rather, this is when all the hard work you've already done is most likely to pay off. If you deserve a raise or promotion, or if you've been working hard toward a specific goal, this is the time in 2025 when you're most likely to see results. (If things don't pan out just yet, don't worry! Saturn will return to Aries in early 2026.)

Uranus, planet of rebellion and innovation, spends most of 2025 in Taurus (though it dips into Gemini from July 7th through November 7th). Uranus first entered Taurus in 2018, and since then, you've probably been experiencing changes— maybe radical ones!—in your plans for the future. Maybe you're rebelling against other people's expectations for you, maybe new people have broadened your horizons, maybe you're simply rethinking your own ideas about what your life should look like. Let this transit remind you that you deserve to dream big and you don't have to settle.

Finally, slow-moving **Pluto** is still in the middle of a yearslong transit through Aquarius that won't end until 2043. More than any of the other outer planets, Pluto's effects tend to be felt collectively more than personally (the exception would be if it connects with a point in your natal chart). For you, Cancer, Pluto is moving through your solar eighth house, so if Pluto does connect with points in your natal chart, it's likely to highlight themes of transformation and rebirth.

Your Ruling Planet

As a Cancer, you're ruled by the Moon: moody, emotive, and mysterious. The Moon is the fastest-moving of all the astrological planets, spending only a few days at a time in each sign, and completing an entire zodiac cycle each month. This means that, even if you don't show it, your moods and desires are constantly changing, and even a challenging lunar transit won't get you down for long. It also means that you're particularly well equipped to make the most of positive lunar transits! This year, pay particular attention to the days when the Moon and Jupiter align in Cancer: June 25th, July 23rd, August 19th, September 16th, October 13th, November 10th, and December 7th. These should all be very lucky days for you. If you need to take a risk, ask someone out, or schedule an important meeting, you won't go wrong with these dates! If you feel like you need a new beginning, the Cancer New Moon on June 25th is one of the best days possible this year for setting fresh intentions.

January

The year 2025 begins with three planets (Mars, Jupiter, and Uranus) retrograde. For you, Cancer, pay particular attention to Mars, which moves into your sign on the 6th. During this time, you'll be filled with passion, ideas, and confidence, but you may struggle to find a way to put it all into action! Don't try to force it: the pieces will fall into place by the time Mars stations direct next month. Mercury will be in Capricorn from the 8th to the 27th: this is an excellent time to sort out relationship problems.

Moon Cycles

The first major lunar event of 2025 is the Full Moon in Cancer on January 13th. You'll likely experience this Moon particularly intensely, and any hidden feelings or emotional needs will be impossible to deny. Be brave enough to ask for support if you need it.

Then on the 29th, the New Moon in Aquarius offers you a rare opportunity to reinvent yourself. If you aren't happy with the way life has been going—or the way you've been acting—you can use this lunar energy to change course and begin a new phase in your life.

Power Days

The 12th brings incredibly romantic energy into your life (just be careful who you share it with while Mars is retrograde!). On the 25th, the more direct you are about your feelings, the more likely you are to get what you want. The 28th is an amazing day to take a chance on love.

Days to Watch For

It's easy to let your temper get the better of you on the 7th: try to control yourself (especially at work). Expect some relationship tension on the 13th: focus on compromise, not winning! Your head and your heart may come into conflict on the 23rd, so don't force yourself to make a decision if you're just not ready.

February

Venus moves into Aries on the 4th, making this month an amazing time to turn on the charm at work. Whether you want to impress the higher-ups, resolve conflict with a colleague, or ask your boss for a raise, you can do it with grace and style—and probably get what you want. On the 23rd, Mars stations direct in Cancer, giving you a nice confidence boost. This is a time to stand up for yourself and to go for what you really want—no holding back.

Moon Cycles

A Full Moon in Leo lights up the sky on the 12th, inviting you to be generous with people in your life. This isn't a time to hold back. If you love someone, tell them. If you have help to offer, then do. The more generous you are, the happier you'll be.

Then on the 27th, a New Moon in Pisces opens the door to new possibilities. Right now, you're hungry for knowledge and experience, and you want to escape your everyday routines. Don't blow up your whole life, but do give yourself permission to explore.

Power Days

Focus on making progress toward your dreams on the 9th: you've got the ambition and dedication to get what you want. The 19th is a good day to *be assertive*: you won't get what you want if you never ask for it! On the 23rd, you can make important decisions with confidence and a clear head.

Days to Watch For

Try to avoid arguments on the 3rd: it's going to be harder than usual to come to a constructive solution. On the 7th, expect to feel some conflict between your duty to others and your personal desires. You may be especially irritable on the 16th: do your best to avoid causing harm.

March

This is a busy month, astrologically speaking! In addition to the eclipses (see more below), Venus and Mercury both station retrograde (on the 1st and 15th, respectively). As much as possible, take things *slow* right now. Be extra careful to back up important files at work (and make sure you're not using work devices for anything you wouldn't want the IT department to see!). Be prepared for miscommunications—both at work and in your relationships—and try not to take them personally. Remember that you don't have to be perfect; you just have to do your best.

Moon Cycles

The first eclipse of 2025 is the lunar eclipse in Virgo on March 14th. Under this eclipse, expect to learn, have deep conversations, and possibly change your mind about something (or someone) in your life. Don't try to take action yet; just keep your mind and your heart open to change.

On the 29th, the solar eclipse in Aries is an invitation into a new era of your professional life. You might get a surprising job offer or an opportunity to do something new. Think carefully and be intentional about what kind of changes you want to make.

Power Days

The 7th is an amazing day for beginning new projects or relationships: your courage and confidence make anything possible. On the 8th, stand up for yourself: you know your worth! Love is in the air on the 22nd: you may even meet someone through work (whether that's a coworker, a client, or someone who works in the same building).

Days to Watch For

You might face some kind of family conflict on the 16th: do your best to stay open-minded as you work it out. Old insecurities may cause fresh problems on the 26th, but with a little compassion for yourself, you'll be fine. The 30th isn't the best day for impulsive decisions: things probably won't turn out the way you wanted.

April

Travel may be a bit dicey until Mercury retrograde ends on the 7th, so build in lots of extra time if you're making travel plans for the first part of this month. Venus retrograde ends on the 12th, so love and relationships should get smoother. (If you're planning on changing your hairstyle, getting a new tattoo, or dropping lots of money on new clothes this month, it's safest to wait until *after* the 12th.) Great news: after the 12th, there are no retrogrades for the rest of April!

Moon Cycles

On the 12th, the Full Moon in Libra may stir up drama within your family (and especially with your parents). While you may prefer to avoid conflict, sharing your feelings and having an honest conversation will probably be better in the long run.

Then on the 27th, a New Moon in Taurus gives you an opportunity to think about the future. Are you happy with your routines and your everyday life, or do you wish things were different? If you need a change, set fresh intentions now—and follow through on them.

Power Days

On the 5th, your instincts—*especially* about the people you encounter—should be spot-on, so trust yourself. Schedule a date for the 6th: it'll be sexy, sweet, and fun. If you've been wanting to discuss a raise or promotion—or to have any other kind of tricky conversation at work—the 25th is a great day to go for it.

Days to Watch For

It's easy to feel insecure on the 3rd: feel your feelings, but don't let them guide your decision-making just now! No matter how cranky you feel on the 13th, try not to lash out at the people you love. You may feel a little paranoid on the 18th, especially at work, but don't read too much into any interactions.

May

While Mercury is in Taurus this month—from the 10th to the 25th—make a point of socializing with your friends or participating in any clubs or groups you're a member of. (It's a particularly good time to throw a dinner party!) If you're having problems, conversations with your friends are the best place to find clarity right now. On the 24th, Saturn enters Aries, where it'll stay until September. Don't be surprised if you get good career news now: your hard work is finally paying off.

Moon Cycles

Under the Scorpio Full Moon on the 12th, you may struggle with some inner conflict: do you want to share your emotions or keep them hidden? While sharing them might be scary right now, it'll lead to stronger relationships (especially in your love life).

You may feel hypersensitive under the New Moon in Gemini on the 26th and find it hard to trust the people around you. But if you can open up to someone who cares about you, they can help you discover important new insights about yourself.

Power Days

If you need to have a tough conversation, the 3rd is an excellent day to do it. You may meet someone new on the 17th: don't be scared to ask them out, even (especially) if they're not your usual type! And if that doesn't work out, you may meet your perfect match on the 22nd.

Days to Watch For

You may feel lonely on the 1st: avoid the temptation to settle for someone you don't really love. On the 16th, your values might clash with those of someone you're close to: talk it out, but don't sacrifice your principles. You might feel frustrated with your career on the 28th, but trust that you're ultimately moving in the right direction.

June

June is a big month for you, Cancer! In addition to the Sun entering your sign on the 20th, Mercury also enters Cancer on the 8th. With both of these planets in your solar first house, you should feel strong, confident, and at ease with who you are. Even more exciting: Jupiter, the planet of luck, enters Cancer on the 9th, ushering in a new period of good fortune for you. Cultivate good luck by caring for others, trusting in your compassion, and simply being yourself.

Moon Cycles

The Full Moon in Sagittarius on the 11th may illuminate a health issue (or, more likely, just a health anxiety you've been sweating about). Don't let worry control your life, and make a point of focusing on self-care, whatever that means for you.

Then on the 25th, the New Moon in Cancer offers you the potential for deep and genuine healing. You spend so much time nurturing others, but under this Moon, make a point of caring for *yourself* and giving yourself the love you need.

Power Days

Your relationships are steady and strong on the 11th, which makes this a great day to ask for support or favors. The 24th is one of the luckiest days of the year for you, so if you've been dreaming about taking a leap, go for it! Treat others with kindness on the 26th, and they'll be incredibly generous in return.

Days to Watch For

The 4th likely isn't the best day for socializing: work events in particular are likely to feel frustrating and unrewarding. You may feel pessimistic on the 9th, but things probably aren't as bad as you're making them out to be. Any personal challenges you've been dealing with this year are likely to come to a head on the 15th.

July

On the 18th, Mercury stations retrograde in Leo. Since this retrograde is taking place in your solar second house, it's especially important to be careful about major financial transactions and contracts! It's safest to avoid this kind of activity altogether until Mercury stations direct next month, but if it can't wait, then be sure to ask lots of questions and have a trusted friend or advisor review your plan. On the 30th, Venus enters Cancer.

This should be a great time for romance: everyone seems to be attracted to your energy right now.

Moon Cycles

The Capricorn Full Moon on the 10th shines a spotlight on your close relationships. If you're in a relationship, make a point of spending quality time with your partner. If you're looking for love, there's a good chance you'll meet your next partner under this Moon.

On the 24th, the New Moon in Leo is a good time to think about your finances. Especially if you feel out of control with your spending, this is an opportunity to focus, create a plan, and make sure you're using money in ways that will actually bring you happiness.

Power Days

Trust your intuition on the 4th, even if it doesn't initially make rational sense. The 15th is a great day for making new friends, especially ones who can help you see the world differently. The 16th is a great day for making plans that are bold and ambitious—but also realistic and achievable.

Days to Watch For

Long-simmering tensions, especially with family members or old friends, could come to the surface on the 2nd: be prepared to finally set things right. The demands of your career might come into conflict with those of your close relationships on the 9th. Expect lots of small conflicts on the 17th, and be prepared to deal with them.

August

Mercury retrograde ends on the 11th, and you can stop being *quite* so cautious about money matters. In fact, this should be a great time for saving, negotiating, and investing in activities and experiences that will make you and your loved ones happy. This becomes even more true when Venus enters Leo on the 25th! Good financial opportunities should come your way—just be careful not to be *too* extravagant. It's a good time to spend money on the things that are genuinely important to you, but don't blow your budget!

Moon Cycles

If you've felt a transformation brewing in your life this year, it'll probably come into focus under the Full Moon in Aquarius on the 9th. You may have a life-changing encounter with somebody new: lean into the change and let the magic happen.

Then on the 23rd, the New Moon in Virgo is all about learning. Whether from reading, or conversation, or just observing the world around you, you can get a deeper understanding of yourself, and what you want, and how to find true happiness.

Power Days

The 11th should be one of the most romantic days of the year: if you put yourself out there, you'll attract the love you need. Increased charm and popularity on the 19th make this a great day for socializing. The 20th is a great day for changing your look (for instance, with a new hairstyle).

Days to Watch For

Any issues with low self-esteem will be exacerbated on the 1st: make self-love a priority. Relationships may face trouble on the 5th, especially if you and your partner have different expectations: clear communication should help. It'll be harder than usual to connect with others on the 18th, but trust that you'll feel like yourself again soon.

September

On the 1st of the month, Saturn moves backward from Aries into Pisces, and work may become less of a priority than it has been for much of this year. Better, for now, to focus on *yourself*, and what kind of person you want to be in the world. Then Mercury enters Libra on the 18th, followed by the Sun on the 22nd. With both of these important planets in your solar fourth house, this is an ideal time for resolving issues with close family members—or simply for spending time with them.

Moon Cycles

The Pisces lunar eclipse arrives on the 7th and may take you away from your usual routines. Expect surprises! Don't try to hold on to things exactly as they are: if you can go with the flow and embrace change, the universe will reward you.

Then with the Virgo solar eclipse on the 21st, new information may come into your life that changes everything. Uncovering secrets, listening to your friends' stories, or diving deep into a new topic may give you the answers you've been looking for and show you a new way forward.

Power Days

Stepping outside of your ordinary routines on the 7th will bring good luck and positive interactions. The 12th is a perfect day to start new projects, especially ones that require you to work with lots of different people. Your self-confidence absolutely shines on the 16th, and you can do anything you set your mind to.

Days to Watch For

On the 3rd, a bad mood might cause you to say things you'll regret later (especially to your partner, if you're in a relationship), so think before you speak. Pick your battles on the 4th! Avoid getting dragged into conflicts that don't really concern you. Your first impressions may not be that strong on the 29th, so try to withhold judgment for now.

October

For you, this should be an amazing month of creativity and self-expression, as Mercury and the Sun both move into Scorpio and your solar fifth house (on the 6th and 22nd, respectively. If you have a creative job or hobby, you'll want to throw yourself into it with fresh intensity, so make sure to carve out time for that! Pluto, which has been retrograde in Aquarius since May, stations direct on the 13th. This could spell major transformation for your life. It's impossible to avoid change right now, so the best thing to do is accept it and grow through it.

Moon Cycles

You may not usually love attention, but the Aries Full Moon on the 6th could thrust you into the spotlight. Be prepared for everyone to be up in your business! Don't try to hide away (it won't work), but instead, try to accept whatever attention comes your way without shame.

Then on the 21st, the New Moon in Libra may be the right time to retreat from the world and spend some quiet time with yourself. Life's been exhausting lately, and you deserve a chance to regroup, recharge, and find your balance again.

Power Days

On the 5th, you have the emotional stability you need to believe in yourself and take big risks. The 24th is a great day to plan for the future, so dream big! Be decisive on the 27th! When you move with confidence and self-assurance, things will turn out well for you.

Days to Watch For

On the 1st, make a point of being humble and considerate in conversation with others—it's easy to accidentally come across as arrogant right now! On the 16th, watch out for overconfidence. On the 28th, other people may be tempted to meddle in your business and relationships if you're not *very* clear about your boundaries.

November

The last of this year's three Mercury retrogrades takes place this month, from the 9th to the 29th. For you, it'll be especially easy to overlook details: the answer isn't to beat yourself up when you make mistakes, but to accept that some are inevitable right now and to ask for help when you need it. Then Jupiter retrograde in Cancer begins on the 11th. Fortunately, this won't be nearly as difficult as Mercury retrograde: rather, this is a lucky opportunity to reconnect with your purpose and change the course of your life.

Moon Cycles

On the 5th, the Taurus Full Moon could spell changes for your social life. If you've been working on building a social circle, you may finally feel like you belong. On the flip side, if you've outgrown a group you're part of, this might be the time to say goodbye.

On the 20th, the New Moon in Scorpio brings a new depth to your love life. If you've felt disconnected from your partner, this is your chance to become truly close again. If you're single, don't settle for a shallow connection: right now, you need (and deserve!) true, deep love.

Power Days

On the 10th, intuition will guide you to make strong decisions—even if you can't explain your reasoning to anyone else. The 16th brings new opportunities for happiness and success, especially in creative fields. The 26th is an excellent day for finding love, strengthening existing relationships, and making fruitful financial decisions.

Days to Watch For

It's incredibly hard to stay motivated on the 2nd: avoid scheduling important tasks for this day, if possible. It might be hard to know what you really want on the 4th, so don't make any binding commitments for now. Other people may try to take advantage of your generosity on the 24th: it's okay to demand fairness in your relationships.

December

The last month of 2025 shines a spotlight on your close relationships. When Mars enters Capricorn on the 15th, you may have conflict with a partner or best friend—but if you treat each other with care and honesty, the experience will ultimately bring you closer together. When the Sun enters Capricorn on the 21st, spending one-on-one time with people you love will teach you a lot about who *you* want to be. Finally, Venus enters Capricorn on the 24th, inviting you to connect with others on a deeper level and find the love you've been missing.

Moon Cycles

Under the Gemini Full Moon on the 4th, you have the chance to release insecurities and old baggage. With the help of the people in your life, you've grown *so* much this year—so don't be ashamed of the past, just keep moving forward.

Under the Sagittarius New Moon on the 19th, you may find yourself wanting to "fix" other people's lives. Try to resist the impulse! Focus instead on making the changes you want to see in your *own* life. It's a perfect time to look to the future and plan new adventures.

Power Days

Trust yourself to make important decisions on the 7th: your instincts are good and your values are solid. The 24th is a beautiful day for all kinds of love and connection: family, friendship, and romance alike. The 29th should be a sweet and romantic day: give yourself permission to enjoy it!

Days to Watch For

It's easy to spend way too much money on the 1st: watch your budget! Emotions could spiral out of control on the 6th: you'll feel better if you talk things through with someone you trust. On the 21st, you're likely to stress yourself out about the future (especially the future of your relationship): avoid the temptation to do something drastic!

Leo

The Lion
July 22 to August 23

Element: Fire
Ruling planet: Sun
Keyword: Proud
Key phrase: I lead

Gemstone: Ruby
Power stones: Topaz, garnet, tiger's-eye
Color: Gold
Flower: Sunflower

All about Leo

Strengths and Gifts

Leo, the lion, arrives in the heart of summertime, and fittingly, it's ruled by the Sun: warm, noble, and generous. A fire sign through and through, Leo is brave, passionate, and full of energy. You're driven by a deep affection for others: you want to make the people in your life happy, and you want to be appreciated for all that you do.

Represented by the regal lion, you, Leo, are a natural-born leader. You have strong feelings about how things "should" be, and you're more than happy to take charge in order to make it happen. In your friend group, you're often the one who takes the lead in making fun happen. At work, you're probably great at motivating and encouraging others. You just care deeply about getting things done and making the world a better place, and you're happy to step up to the plate and take charge— especially when nobody else seems to be stepping in.

Your leadership skills *may* sometimes come across as just a bit bossy, but you don't intend to be authoritarian! In fact, Leos are among the most caring and generous people out there. You just have high standards (both for other people *and* for yourself), strong principles, and clear ideas about how to improve the world. You're not someone to be satisfied by mediocre work or half-assed efforts. From work to relationships, you give 100 percent, and you expect other people to do the same. You're proud of the work you do in the world and the effort you put into your relationships, and you want your effort to be recognized!

This means that, while some people can't stand being the center of attention, you're the opposite: you *love* the spotlight! When you feel seen, recognized, and appreciated is when you truly come alive. (And when you give your attention and appreciation to others, they probably come alive, too!) This doesn't necessarily mean that you're always the life of the party or that you love to literally be on stage (though lots of actors are Leos!). The important thing, in whatever field you work in or whatever setting you find yourself in, is that you're given consideration, that your achievements are praised and recognized, and that you don't feel taken for granted.

Friendship and Love

You have a *lot* of affection to share, which means that relationships are a top priority. For you, giving and receiving love makes life worth living! In relationships, you're probably not one to waste time with someone you're not sure about or to tolerate anyone who keeps you guessing about how they really feel. You're an absolute catch, Leo, and you deserve to be with someone who recognizes this! You want to absolutely adore the person you're with, and to be adored in return.

In both friendship and romance, you probably have high standards for the people you allow into your inner circle. Once someone's in, though, they're *in*: you're loyal and true to the people you've chosen, and you'll do virtually anything to make those you love happy. You understand that relationships of all kinds require care and attention, and you make a point of actively investing in yours. From kind words to thoughtful gifts to planning dates or group get-togethers, you do what you can to *show* people how much you care.

In return, you expect others to show *you* the same care and consideration—and you'll quickly get offended if you feel you're being taken for granted. You thrive on praise, attention, and admiration. When people think you're beautiful or interesting or cool, you want them to *say so*! Because of your confidence and larger-than-life personality, other people sometimes assume that you don't need to hear their compliments—but the fact is, you do, and you might need to remind them of that!

Sometimes your ideas about how the world (and the people in it) "should" be can get a little rigid, and this may cause trouble in your relationships. When you and your partner have different needs, expectations, or communication styles, you often imagine that one of you must be doing something wrong. Try to remember that it's okay for people to be different, as long as you're communicating and treating each other with kindness.

Work and Money

Many Leos love to work in the spotlight—but this doesn't mean that all Leos crave fame! Far from it. There are lots of ways to be seen and noticed: giving talks at conferences, training new employees at your job, being a tour guide, or even bartending at the coolest new spot in town could all scratch that itch. But no matter what field you end up working in, you've got a lot to offer—and the most important thing is that you work somewhere that recognizes that, and gives you space and encouragement to shine.

When it comes to money, your keyword is generosity! You're probably the type of person who'd spend your last dollar to help a friend or to buy your partner the perfect birthday gift. (You're generous with yourself, too. If you find the perfect eye-catching outfit to wear to a big event, you won't be dissuaded just because it's outside your budget.) This is one of the loveliest things about you! But try to remember that you don't need to spend big or buy extravagant gifts to show your love: the people in your life love you for *you*.

Struggles and Growth

Your confidence and big personality may disguise your deep need for love! Other people don't always recognize your vulnerable, sensitive side—they may even feel intimidated by you—and so they might not treat you as gently as you need. This can lead to misunderstandings, conflict, and heartbreak. The key here, for you, is to learn how to set aside your pride and actually *express* your needs to the people in your life! Don't assume they know what you want or how you need to be loved. It may seem obvious to you, but sometimes you have to state it plainly.

You can also occasionally get a bit rigid in your ideas about the world. On the one hand, this is a wonderful thing: it means you have a lot of integrity and stand firm in your principles. But you can grow and strengthen your relationships by keeping an open heart, being willing to learn, and changing your mind every once in a while.

Journaling Page

Think about your goals for 2025. Which of your Leo gifts—leadership, confidence, generosity, warmth—will you call on to help you achieve them? Which elements of the Leo personality do you want to lean into this year?

The Year Ahead for Leo

The Eclipses

If you want to be ready for the big story (and big dramas!) of 2025, one of the best ways to start is by looking at the eclipses. Every year has them, and they mark the major pivot points of the year. You won't necessarily feel every eclipse equally: your personal birth chart will determine which eclipses feel like fireworks and which pass by without notice. But it's always worth paying attention to the eclipses, even the ones that affect you in subtler ways. The year 2025 has four eclipses: lunar eclipses in Virgo and Pisces and solar eclipses in Aries and Virgo.

The first is the lunar eclipse in Virgo, which happens on March 14th. During this eclipse, you may experience excitement surrounding money, finances, or material possessions. You could finally get a raise, or an unexpected windfall might fall into your lap. This is also an excellent time to declutter your living space, getting rid of what you no longer want or need.

Then on March 29th, a solar eclipse in Aries offers you a doorway to adventure. If your life has gotten stagnant, count on this eclipse to shake things up again. You don't have to go out of your way to find excitement—trust that the universe will bring you just the opportunity you've been looking for.

September brings the final two eclipses of 2025. On the 7th, a lunar eclipse in Pisces is likely to bring intense emotional experiences—maybe even intense spiritual experiences. This eclipse should illuminate what's *truly* important to you. You may be surprised by what you learn about yourself, but keep an open heart.

Finally, the last eclipse of the year—this time a solar eclipse in Virgo—falls on September 21st. This one is a chance for you to set a new financial course for yourself. Maybe unexpected opportunities will become available, or maybe you'll finally feel empowered to handle things differently.

The Big Picture

The eclipses may be important, but they're far from the only important information the skies hold about your year ahead. The next place to look is the outer planets of Jupiter, Saturn, Uranus, Neptune, and Pluto. These planets move slowly through the zodiac, and their effects can be far-reaching, defining months (sometimes years) of our lives.

To get a sense of what kind of luck you'll have in the year ahead, keep an eye on **Jupiter**, which spends roughly half of 2025 in Gemini before moving into Cancer on June 9th, where it'll stay for the rest of the year. While Jupiter is in Gemini, focus on your friendships and social circle: even the smallest interactions with others right now will hold the potential to change your life for the better! Then, once Jupiter enters Cancer, focus on expanding your spiritual life, your emotional resources, or your compassion for yourself. If you're like most Leos, you're probably happiest among other people—but let Jupiter in Cancer inspire you to enjoy your own company, too.

Saturn, planet of discipline and responsibility, will spend 2025 in Pisces and Aries. It starts the year in Pisces, moves into Aries on May 24th, then returns to Pisces on September 1st. During its time in free-flowing Pisces, you're likely to struggle some with the changes happening in your life: it feels harder than ever to balance structure with freedom, stability with growth. Do your best not to be *too* resistant to change—your life can transform for the better, but only if you let it! When Saturn moves into Aries, you'll get a taste of that transformation. Take practical steps to learn and expand your mind (Sign up for a class! Plan a trip!), and you'll see amazing results.

Dreamy **Neptune** also spends 2025 in Pisces and Aries. While it moves through Pisces (the beginning of the year to March 30th, and October 22nd through the end of the year), you may forge a deep, soulmate-level romantic or sexual connection—but you'll also have a harder time discerning if a new partner is too good to be true. Enjoy the sweet vibes, but take things *slow* and keep your head on your shoulders!

Unpredictable **Uranus**, planet of change and rebelliousness, spends much of 2025 in Taurus (though it dips into Gemini from July 7th through November 7th). This is the continuation of a story that started when Uranus first entered Taurus back in 2018; during this time, you've likely experienced career shake-ups (or maybe just conflict with your boss!). But once it enters Gemini this year (and again, for the long haul, in 2026), your focus will shift. This is a time to meet exciting new people, participate in different social scenes, or make bold choices that might surprise your friends. On July 23rd in particular you should find it easy to seize your freedom and live big.

Finally, slow-moving **Pluto** is still in the middle of a yearslong transit through Aquarius that won't end until 2043. Pluto is the planet of transformation and rebirth, and for you in particular this is likely to be felt in the realm of your close relationships and partnerships. Don't let this scare you! This is simply a time to make any necessary changes so you can feel truly fulfilled in your relationships. (Heads up: the biggest transformations are likely to occur on or around July 25th, when the Sun and Pluto are opposite each other in the zodiac.)

Your Ruling Planet

The Sun is incredibly important to *everybody's* astrological outlook, but especially yours, Leo, as it's your ruling planet. (Since the Sun is at the center of the solar system, it makes perfect sense that you're so comfortable being the center of attention!) This means that, unlike all the other signs except for Cancer, you never have to deal with your ruling planet going retrograde, since the Sun never moves backward through the zodiac. It also means that the time when the Sun is in Leo (in other words, your birthday season!) is an especially fruitful time of year for you, so make sure to celebrate yourself. This year, July 24th may end up being one of the biggest days of the year for you, as the Sun in Leo harmonizes with Saturn and Neptune and opposes Pluto. July 31st, when the Sun and Mercury align in Leo, is an excellent day for making plans for your year ahead.

♌

January

The year begins with three retrograde planets: Jupiter, Uranus, and Mars. Mars is likely to be the most troublesome of these three—especially for you, since it's in Leo until the 6th. During this time, try to avoid taking any unnecessary risks, and be aware that conflict could get started more easily than usual, so be mindful of how you interact with those around you. As long as you manage your expectations and act with a little extra care and intentionality, you'll be just fine.

Moon Cycles

The year's first major lunar event is the Full Moon in Cancer on January 13th. This Moon has the potential to heal some old wounds and deep-seated insecurities. In order to make the most of it, be sure to schedule some alone time for rest and reflection.

Then on the 29th, the New Moon in Aquarius is an ideal time to meet people and begin new relationships. Especially if you've been dissatisfied with your social circle or love life in the past, now is your opportunity to turn over a new leaf and try a different approach.

Power Days

Your charm and leadership qualities are on full display on the 5th: don't be afraid to step up! If you've been having relationship troubles, you'll be able to get to the bottom of things on the 21st. The 28th is a great day for clear, open communication with those you love: no secrets!

Days to Watch For

Your competitive nature is activated on the 2nd: fight for what you want, but be careful not to unnecessarily hurt others' feelings. On the 3rd, other people might take advantage of you unless you stand up for yourself. Watch out for relationship drama (especially based in jealousy) on the 14th.

February

When Venus moves into Aries on the 4th, expect your love life to get spicier! This doesn't necessarily signal drama—it just means that romance is likely to surprise you, challenge your preexisting beliefs, or invite you to look at the world through a different lens. If you're in a committed relationship already, this is a great time to go on a trip together. Mars retrograde ends on the 23rd, giving you a confidence boost! If you've been holding off on beginning a new adventure, you can take the plunge now.

Moon Cycles

The 12th brings a Full Moon in your home sign of Leo! Make a point of asserting yourself today—*especially* if you've felt overlooked or underappreciated lately. (Just be careful not to trample on other people's feelings while you stand up for your own.)

Then on the 27th, the New Moon in Pisces is an ideal moment to open up and share how you're feeling. It isn't easy to let your defenses fall, but right now it can deepen your existing relationships—and might even help you understand yourself better.

Power Days

Contracts, business dealings, legal matters, and negotiations of all kinds are likely to go well for you on the 3rd. The 9th is a great day for meeting new people, whether professional contacts, friends, or potential partners. Honesty is the best policy on the 25th: the more open you are, the stronger your relationships will be.

Days to Watch For

The smallest things can set off arguments on the 4th: do your best to keep your cool (especially at work). Unwanted changes may loom on the 11th, but if you lean into them, things might turn out for the best after all. It's easy to feel like you're being pushed around on the 12th: look for a compromise.

March

Venus retrograde begins on the 1st, which could signal a frustrating time in your love life. If things aren't working right now, it's probably not you—it's just bad timing. (And remember that it's always wise to avoid changing up your look in a dramatic way while Venus, planet of beauty, is retrograde!) Mercury retrograde starts on the 15th and will last until April 7th. If you're traveling, have a backup plan or two in place: problems and delays are especially likely between the 14th and 29th.

Moon Cycles

The first eclipse of 2025 is here! On the 14th, the lunar eclipse in Virgo will invite you to examine your values, and the ways you want to put them into practice. What *really* matters to you? With this in mind, how will you direct your energy?

Then on the 29th, the solar eclipse in Aries makes you feel incredibly restless: you're ready for new people, new places, new adventures! The key right now is to remember that you're in the driver's seat. So if it's time for a change, go for it.

Power Days

The 10th is a great day for romance—or maybe for discovering that a friendship might have the potential for something more. Don't underestimate the power of a little mystery on the 23rd: leave people wanting more! The 24th gives your confidence a boost, and you can take major steps toward your goals.

Days to Watch For

Avoid making any last-minute changes to your plans on the 11th: while it might seem like a good idea, it probably won't work out. Keep your composure and try not to get drawn into a power struggle on the 17th. Your instincts are usually sound—but before you do anything drastic on the 26th, get a second opinion.

April

There's lots of good news for you this month! First, Mercury retrograde ends on the 7th. Communication with people close to you should be smoother now, and your own thinking will feel clearer, too. Then on the 12th, Venus retrograde ends as well (and after this, *no* planets are retrograde for the rest of the month!). On the 18th, Mars moves into Leo again, making you confident, powerful, and ready to stand up for yourself. This is a *great* time for progressing toward your goals and getting things done!

Moon Cycles

Under the Full Moon in Libra on the 12th, life is probably getting *busy*. Your workdays are jam-packed and your social calendar is full. Focus on finding balance, and remember that you don't have to do things just because others want you to.

The Taurus New Moon on the 27th is an amazing time to set new goals and intentions for your career. Think about where you'd like to be a few years from now, and harness your confidence and determination to start making moves to get there.

Power Days

Sharing your own unique insights on the 1st can lead to major successes at work. Trust your instincts on the 4th: if you start a new venture or take a calculated risk right now, it's *very* likely to pay off. Conversations with friends on the 7th will be especially illuminating and may help you decide on next steps.

Days to Watch For

Expect relationship drama on the 6th—but it'll blow over soon, so just focus on keeping your cool and not making things worse. Other people's (especially bosses' or colleagues') egos might cause problems for you on the 20th, but compromise is better than conflict right now. If you feel frustrated and discouraged on the 26th, ask your friends for help.

May

Pluto retrograde begins on the 4th, but don't worry! This won't be as stressful or intense as the Mercury, Venus, and Mars retrogrades you've already experienced this year. Think of this as a time for you to dig deep into your closest relationships: Are you getting what you need? Are you happy with the person you are in these relationships? If something's not right, this retrograde invites you to be honest about that, and to think about how you might create a change.

Moon Cycles

You may experience some family drama or home maintenance issues under the Scorpio Full Moon on the 12th. Don't hesitate to put all your energies toward dealing with the problem. You deserve to feel comfortable, happy, and balanced at home.

Then the Gemini Moon on the 26th is an absolutely ideal time to broaden your social network! If you meet someone new right now, they could introduce you to new ideas, connect you to a new group, or change the course of your life for the better.

Power Days

Your intuition is sharper than ever on the 3rd, so trust yourself (even if there's no rational explanation!). The 14th is a great day to schedule job interviews, client meetings, or first dates: you'll make an amazing first impression. If you're looking for love, the 22nd is a great day for finding someone you genuinely hit it off with.

Days to Watch For

Simmering tensions may come to the surface on the 4th: you'll be better off dealing with the situation head-on than avoiding it. It's easy to feel like others aren't appreciating you enough at work on the 12th, but try not to get defensive. On the 17th, think before you speak, or you're likely to rub people the wrong way.

June

On the 6th, Venus moves into Taurus, ushering in a harmonious time at work. Relationships with colleagues, clients, and even your boss should be easy and rewarding now. This is also a great time to redecorate your work space. On the 17th, Mars leaves Leo to enter Virgo. Watch your spending right now! Buying new things won't actually change your life (though it's easy to feel like it will). On the 26th, Mercury moves into Leo: this is an ideal time for self-reflection and for expressing your unique point of view to others.

Moon Cycles

The Sagittarius Full Moon on the 11th is a particularly lovely one for you: this is your time to shine! Carve out some time for self-expression, creativity, and play. Life doesn't have to be so serious all the time. You deserve to have fun, too.

Then on the 25th, use the Cancer New Moon to get some alone time and recharge your batteries. You might feel especially tired now—don't try to fight it! Instead, give yourself all the time you need to rest, reflect, and regroup.

Power Days

If you've been waiting to ask your crush out, the 1st is an ideal day to go for it (just don't get pushy!). The 21st is a beautiful day for dates, parties, and social get-togethers of all kinds—

even (and maybe especially) work networking events. You can find a *lot* of wisdom by asking others for advice on the 27th.

Days to Watch For

Watch your temper on the 8th! It's going to be incredibly easy to hurt loved ones' feelings by accident. The 15th is *not* a great day for risk-taking behaviors, no matter how much you feel the urge to act out. Be careful with your money on the 28th: it's all too easy to create problems for yourself by overspending.

July

The second of this year's three Mercury retrogrades starts on the 18th. This one takes place entirely in the sign of Leo, so you may feel it personally! Be prepared to feel a bit misunderstood while this retrograde is going on, and to give yourself some extra care and compassion. On the bright side, the Sun enters Leo on the 22nd! This is a time to focus on *you*: to advocate for yourself, to give yourself credit for everything you've accomplished over the past year, or to set ambitious goals for the year ahead.

Moon Cycles

On the 10th, the Full Moon in Capricorn helps you to see your habits and routines with clarity—and understand what's not working for you anymore. This is a great opportunity to get rid of bad habits and replace them with ones that are (physically *or* emotionally) healthier.

If you've been wanting to change your life or reinvent yourself, the Leo New Moon on the 24th is one of the best days of the year for it. It can be scary to try something new, but if you believe in yourself and trust your heart, you won't go wrong.

Power Days

The 18th is a great day for doing favors for your friends—and receiving favors and goodwill in return. Patience, determination, and hard work are your best friends on the 24th: with a little persistence, you can do practically anything. The busier your social calendar is on the 31st, the more excitement and opportunities will enter your life.

Days to Watch For

It could be difficult to keep a clear head on the 5th, but do your best to stay unbiased. You may struggle to make sense of your feelings (particularly romantic ones) on the 12th, so avoid making big decisions for now. Unexpected changes are likely around the 25th, but while they won't be easy, they can transform your life for the better.

August

First things first: Mercury retrograde ends on the 11th! If you've had a tougher time than usual expressing your ideas or emotions, you should feel more like your usual self now. On the 22nd, the Sun leaves Leo and enters Virgo: this is a time for you to focus on your finances and think about whether it might be time to make a change. Finally, on the 25th, Venus enters Leo! You'll probably feel extra attractive and charming right now (and others will notice, too!), so make the most of it.

Moon Cycles

Under the Aquarius Full Moon on the 9th, you may experience a bit of stress about your relationship with a partner or best friend. Spend time together and talk through any misunderstandings, and you'll end up even closer than you were before.

On the 23rd, the New Moon in Virgo is a great time to set fresh money goals or to create a detailed budget (and stick to it!). Any work you do now to figure out your financial situation will pay off in a big way down the line.

Power Days

If you're been experiencing misunderstandings in any relationships, the 3rd is a great day for sorting things out. The 17th is an ideal time for finally getting to all the difficult tasks on your to-do list that you've been putting off. Forget about playing the field on the 25th: this is a good time to commit for the long term.

Days to Watch For

Try to keep your head on straight on the 1st: if you rely on feelings alone, you can easily be misled. You may feel like your needs and your partners' needs aren't aligning on the 9th: don't get defensive, just communicate. If problems arise on the 15th, just stay calm and deal with them one at a time.

September

Both Mercury and Venus leave Leo and enter Virgo this month: Mercury on the 2nd, and Venus on the 19th. With both planets entering your solar second house of money, material possessions, and values, this is an excellent time to track your spending, set a new budget, or invest in things that will make your day-to-day life easier. On the 22nd, Mars enters Scorpio, and it could signal conflict with your family or the people you live with. Make an extra effort to understand where they're coming from, and you'll be okay.

Moon Cycles

It's eclipse season again! The Pisces lunar eclipse arrives on the 7th to stir things up in your relationships. As much as you might try to hide your feelings, they'll probably all come to light now, so be honest with the people you care about—even when it's hard.

The Virgo solar eclipse on the 21st could bring financial surprises your way, from an unexpected raise to a major windfall. Whatever happens, don't lose your head! Stick to your budget and your plans, and you'll be in good shape for the future.

Power Days

The 9th is a deeply romantic day for you: confessions of love and grand gestures are likely to go over well! Let your confidence shine on the 15th: the more you show you believe in yourself, the more others will be drawn to you, too. On the 17th, listen to your inner voice.

Days to Watch For

Differences between you and your partner or crush are likely to be accentuated on the 5th: stay kind as you sort through things. It could be hard to be motivated on the 11th, so try not to schedule important tasks or deadlines for the day. On the 24th, others may try to intimidate you: don't let them!

October

Mercury enters Scorpio on the 6th, followed by the Sun on the 22nd. With both of these planets in intense and brooding Scorpio (and your solar fourth house) you have a great opportunity now to reflect on memories and innermost thoughts—maybe even to get a little nostalgic. If you feel less outgoing than usual, lean into it! We all need a break from the hustle and bustle every once in a while. (Once Mercury enters Sagittarius on the 29th, things should change. This marks the start of a fun and creative time of year for you!)

Moon Cycles

Ready or not, the Aries Full Moon on the 6th might push you to take a leap of faith. This isn't the time to be conservative or stick with tradition; rather, it's your chance to follow your heart, trust the universe, and try something totally new.

Then on the 21st, the New Moon in Libra is a nice moment for enjoying yourself. You don't have to do anything big or brave right now—just explore your neighborhood, meet new people, and focus on finding beauty in the everyday world around you.

Power Days

The 1st could bring exciting interactions and chance encounters, especially with people outside your usual circle. You'll have to control your temper on the 23rd (especially with family members!), but if you do, you can accomplish amazing things. Take the initiative on the 27th, even if you're nervous, and things will go your way.

Days to Watch For

Gossip and secrets (maybe your own) could come to light on the 7th, so it's more important than ever to act with kindness and good intentions. Your feelings could get tangled up on the 8th, so talk things through with someone you trust. Keep your ego under control on the 24th! Cooperation will work better than power games right now.

November

The final Mercury retrograde of 2025 happens this month, from the 9th to the 29th. The key right now is simply to *slow down*. If you try to rush through things, you'll probably run into trouble, but if you take it slow and steady, you'll be just fine. The good news for you is that lots of planets are entering Sagittarius and your solar fifth house of creativity and romance: Mars on the 4th, the Sun on the 21st, and Venus on the 30th. Express yourself and have fun!

Moon Cycles

Under the Taurus Full Moon on the 5th, all eyes are on you! At least, that's how it feels. If you've been working hard all year on a particular project or toward a special goal, you're likely to finally get some recognition now. Enjoy it!

Then under the Scorpio New Moon on the 20th, it's all about intimacy. What (or who) makes you feel safe? What do you need to feel truly comfortable in your own skin? Right now, you don't need any big excitement—focus instead on whatever brings you emotional security.

Power Days

Lean into your compassionate side on the 3rd: kindness and generosity will open doors for you today. Be direct on the 10th! The best way to get what you want right now is to ask for it directly. Good fortune is on your side on the 17th—and the harder you work, the more lucky opportunities will come your way.

Days to Watch For

Feelings may get so intense on the 7th that it could be easy to make unwise decisions: before you do anything big, give yourself time to sleep on it. Watch out for petty disagreements on the 11th, and take the high road whenever you can. Expect a little chaos on the 21st! Don't be rigid—try to welcome some change into your life.

December

You have the first half of December to enjoy the lineup of planets in Sagittarius (which Mercury enters on the 11th)—then in the second half of the month, they begin moving into Capricorn:

Mars on the 15th, the Sun on the 21st, and Venus on the 24th. This is a good time to look forward to the future. Don't expect instant gratification right now; instead, focus on helping others and setting yourself up for the days ahead, and you'll be in amazing shape to finish out this year and begin the next.

Moon Cycles

The final Full Moon of 2025 is in Gemini on the 4th, and you'll see how strong all your social connections are. This is a great day to go to a party, run into friends on the street, or be reminded just how many people care about you.

Under the Sagittarius New Moon on the 19th, you're at your most charming and dazzling! This is an excellent time to start a new romance, to meet an amazing new friend, or to begin that passion project you've been dreaming about all year.

Power Days

The 8th is a great day for dating: even ordinary activities will feel *incredibly* romantic. Don't try to blend into the crowd on the 9th: the more you let your authentic self shine, the more others will be drawn to you. Your true emotions about a new friend or crush should become clear on the 17th.

Days to Watch For

Try not to rush things on the 10th: the more you try to speed through your tasks, the more you'll make mistakes. Even if you're frustrated on the 16th, keep working hard: it'll bring back your confidence in no time. Insecurities could flare up on the 23rd, so avoid spending time with people who make you doubt yourself.

♍

Virgo

The Virgin
August 23 to September 22

Element: Earth
Ruling planet: Mercury
Keyword: Thoughtful
Key phrase: I analyze

Gemstone: Sapphire
Power stones: Peridot, amazonite
Color: Navy blue
Flower: Morning glory

All about Virgo

Strengths and Gifts

The Sun moves through Virgo during the last days of summer leading up to the autumn equinox. As an earth sign ruled by Mercury, the planet of thought and communication, Virgo is thoughtful, practical, and detail-oriented. You're driven by a sense of responsibility, a desire to be helpful, and a rare ability to create order out of chaos.

Thanks to your ruling planet of Mercury, you have a razor-sharp intellect. Your skills of observation are top-notch; not much gets past you, Virgo. In fact, you probably register a lot more than other people realize! You're likely the first person to notice when a friend has gotten a new haircut, when a colleague is putting in extra effort, or when an important document contains a typo. Your keen eye makes you a natural editor (even the smallest mistakes and inconsistencies jump out at you!) and a great person to go to for advice. If a friend is dating someone who turns out to be bad news, for instance, you're likely to pick up on the red flags before anybody else.

This doesn't mean you're all criticism and no action! Far from it. As an earth sign, you're all about doing what needs to be done, from keeping your kitchen tidy to keeping work projects running smoothly. It's important to you to be helpful, and if you notice other people dropping the ball, you're more than willing to step in and pick up the slack. In contrast to Leo, the sign immediately before you in the zodiac, you aren't necessarily motivated by a desire for praise. It's *nice* to be recognized, of course, but knowing that you've done good work is its own reward, too.

Your deep inner drive to get things *right* and do good work serves you well in all your pursuits, from career to hobbies to relationships. You're not set in your ways, Virgo, but are always open to learning. If there's a better way of organizing your schedule, you want to learn! If there's a better way of communicating with the people you love, you're all ears. You want to make the world a better place and to be the best version of yourself you can be, and you know that the best way to do this is to keep an open mind and commit to learning and growing.

Friendship and Love

Any person should consider themselves lucky to have a friend or partner like you, Virgo. You're the type to pay attention to what kinds of movies your crush likes, to remember every anniversary and special day, or to make note of your friend's favorite dessert and make it for them when they're having a rough day. Grand gestures are nice, but you understand that the small acts matter, too—maybe even more. You have a gift of observation and put it to excellent use when it comes to caring for the people you love.

You're truly generous with friends and partners. With you, it's never about scoring points or getting credit for your actions; it's satisfying for you simply to know that you've brightened the day or eased the path of someone you love. (Though sometimes you're so focused on making other people happy that you forget to ask whether they're making *you* happy, too. Try to remember that every relationship should be a two-way street!)

One of the ways you show people you care is by pointing out the flaws in their ideas and sharing your ideas about how they could do things better. The problem is that even though you're only trying to be helpful, it can come across as overly critical—even nagging—to others. Just because *you* are typically open to hearing constructive criticism, that doesn't mean other people are the same. You can strengthen your relationships by asking whether it's a good time to share feedback or by couching your ideas in softer language.

With new people, you can be a bit shy; even in settings where you're comfortable, you sometimes feel overlooked in favor of your louder or flashier friends. Maybe you don't naturally call attention to yourself—just remember that you deserve to shine, too! Don't wait around for other people to make all the first moves. You might be surprised by how rewarding it is to practice stepping outside your comfort zone every so often, whether that means dressing to impress, asking your crush out, or making a bold declaration of love.

Work and Money

You truly shine in jobs where you're able to implement structure and create order out of chaos. Building and maintaining organizational systems, managing complex schedules, editing or proofreading pieces of writing, even coding: all of these are kinds of work you might truly excel at. With your ruling planet of Mercury, the key is that you need to be intellectually stimulated at work! Your mind is sharp and busy, and if it isn't challenged, you'll get bored quickly. It's also important to you that your work is meaningful: you thrive most when you're helping people or making the world a better place.

With your keen analytical mind, you're most likely great at budgeting, investing, and managing your finances in an organized fashion. You probably have detailed systems to make sure the bills get paid and your savings account grows. Just remember that life is meant to be enjoyed, too—and that money can help you do that. Remember that you're allowed to spend money on yourself. If you don't have a line item in your budget for the occasional splurge, go ahead and add one!

Struggles and Growth

Your detail-oriented mind is a tremendous gift. It allows you to intercept problems before they happen and to see things that other people miss. The trouble is that sometimes you get *so* focused on the details that you miss the bigger picture! It's possible to dot all your i's and cross all your t's, but miss out on larger opportunities, forget about your long-term goals, or just end up unhappy with your life. Every once in a while, make a point to look up from the small stuff and make sure that things are on track overall.

Occasionally, your desire to get everything right can also present a problem. While it's good to be conscientious, *nobody* can be perfect all the time, no matter how meticulous you are.

It's important that you don't let your perfectionistic side prevent you from experiencing life in all its messy, joyful glory. You'll make some mistakes—everybody does—but you're still worthy of happiness and love.

Journaling Page

Think about your goals for 2025. Which of your Virgo gifts—thoughtfulness, intellect, practicality, organization—will you call on to help you achieve them? Which elements of the Virgo personality do you want to lean into this year?

♍

The Year Ahead for Virgo

The Eclipses

Paying attention to the eclipses is one of the best ways to get ready for what the year ahead has to offer. Eclipses happen every year, and they can point to some of the main plot points—beginnings, endings, and surprising twists—in the story of that year. You won't feel the effects of every eclipse equally—that depends on your personal birth chart. Since two of this year's four eclipses are in your home sign of Virgo, it's especially important to pay attention to them!

First up is the lunar eclipse in Virgo on March 14th. For you, this is a big opportunity—or challenge, depending on how you see it—to assert yourself. If you've been putting everybody else's desires above yours, this is your wake-up call: you deserve to (and need to!) honor your own needs and act like you matter, too.

Then on March 29th, a solar eclipse in Aries marks a new beginning for you. Especially if you've been struggling to figure out what you really want in life, or why you feel the way you do about somebody in your life, this eclipse may offer new clarity—and a path forward that feels surprising but right.

The third and fourth eclipses of the year both happen in September. On the 7th, a lunar eclipse in Pisces may test your relationship with somebody close to you: a partner, best friend, or close colleague. If you can really *listen*—don't assume you know what the other person is thinking!—then you'll ultimately grow closer through the experience.

The final eclipse of the year, just like the first one, happens in Virgo: this one is a solar eclipse, falling on September 21st. This might be your biggest chance all year to reinvent yourself. If you need to turn over a new leaf, commit to a new life path, or simply have some new experiences, this eclipse should empower you to do so.

The Big Picture

For more astrological clues to the overarching story of your year, look to the outer planets of Jupiter, Saturn, Uranus, Neptune, and Pluto. While the inner planets can tell you a lot about your personality, moods, and daily life, these outer planets, which move much more slowly through the zodiac, have a lot to teach about the big picture.

To start, let's take a look at **Jupiter.** This is the planet that can tell you what kind of luck you'll have in the year ahead—and, even better, how you can create your own luck. Jupiter spends roughly the first half of 2025 in Gemini and your solar tenth house of career and reputation. This is great news for you career-wise! Promotions, awards, or exciting career changes are likely right now, and professional networking is likely to pay huge dividends for you. Then on June 9th, Jupiter moves into Cancer, where it'll stay for the rest of the year. Once it does, shift your focus to your friend group. Caring for the people around you will be one of the best ways to create good fortune for yourself.

Saturn, planet of discipline and responsibility, spends the year in Pisces and Aries. It starts out in Pisces, moves into Aries on May 24th, and returns to Pisces on September 1st. While it's in Pisces, your close relationships may be a source of some stress, and your needs or expectations of each other may clash. It's more important than ever to put in the work to overcome any issues—and if you do, your relationship will be stronger than ever. While Saturn is in Aries, you may experience a big, life-changing transformation. Money troubles are possible right now, but with a bit of courage and determination, you'll figure out a new plan—probably one that's even better than the original one.

Neptune, planet of dreams and illusions, also splits its time between Pisces and Aries this year, starting the year in Pisces, entering Aries on March 30th, and returning to Pisces on October 22nd. While it's in Pisces, be extra careful not to put other people (especially crushes or new partners) on a pedestal, or you may be disappointed down the line. When Neptune enters Aries, be on the lookout for scams! If a seemingly amazing investment opportunity presents itself—especially in the world of crypto—do all your due diligence before you commit.

Uranus, the wild child of the solar system, spends much of 2025 in Taurus (though it dips into Gemini from July 7th through November 7th, then moves into Gemini for the long haul in early 2026). It's been in Taurus since 2018, so this is a continuation of a story that's been going on for a while now. With Uranus in Taurus, you've likely been experiencing big (and exciting!) shifts in the way you understand the world. Once Uranus enters Gemini, be prepared for some shake-ups in your career! New opportunities—ones you probably aren't even looking for—are on their way, and it's just up to you to take advantage of them.

Finally, **Pluto**—the most distant and slowest-moving of the planets—continues its yearslong journey through Aquarius, where it'll be until 2043. This year, let Pluto empower you in transforming your daily life: you don't have to keep to the same schedule you always have, or eat the same foods, or stick to the same exercise routine. If something isn't feeling right for you, or if you've outgrown your old habits, then consider this the time to make a change.

Your Ruling Planet

Your ruling planet, Virgo, is Mercury: planet of thought, communication, and connection. This is part of what makes you so perceptive and analytical! It also means you'll want to pay particular attention to this year's three Mercury retrogrades, which run from March 15th to April 7th, July 18th to August 11th, and November 9th to November 29th. During the first retrograde, misunderstandings are likely to crop up, particularly with a partner or best friend: be careful not to jump to conclusions. During the second, you may struggle to express how you're feeling—don't expect yourself to say everything perfectly, just do your best. During the third retrograde, you can expect to run into a scheduling mix-up or two, so make sure to write your appointments down. Mercury retrograde really isn't as scary as people sometimes make it out to be. Just try to take things slow, double-check your work, and most of all, give yourself (and others!) grace when mistakes happen.

♍

January

As 2025 kicks off, there are three retrograde planets: Mars, Jupiter, and Uranus. Jupiter and Uranus shouldn't be too disruptive, but Mars is one to keep an eye on! For you, Virgo, this Mars retrograde makes it easy to feel discouraged, or even to get in your own way. If you've got big New Year's resolutions, think about waiting until next month to set your plans in motion. On the bright side, Venus moves into Pisces on the 2nd, making this month a truly lovely time for strengthening relationships and starting new ones.

Moon Cycles

On January 13th, the Cancer Full Moon fills your life with community. It's an especially good time to help out a friend— or to call on a friend when *you* need help. Caring for the people in your circle will light up your life right now.

Then on the 29th, the Aquarius New Moon is an ideal time to restructure your daily life in order to support your future self. Whether you want to start exercising more, get better sleep, or invest in your relationships, the changes you make now will have big effects down the line.

Power Days

The 3rd is a beautiful day for love and romance: no big drama, just sweetness and good energy. Expect exciting changes to come your way on the 18th. If you're offered an opportunity for adventure, go for it! The 25th is an excellent day to go on a date, maybe even with someone you thought was just a friend.

Days to Watch For

You'll probably be *way* more sensitive than usual on the 6th, so avoid spending time with people who don't make you feel good about yourself. Your judgment could be clouded on the 10th: wait to make important decisions if you can. Be careful not to let jealousy ruin an otherwise strong relationship on the 17th.

February

Venus leaves Pisces to enter Aries on the 4th, but Mercury and the Sun both enter Pisces and your solar seventh house of relationships this month (on the 14th and 18th, respectively). This makes February an ideal time to focus on close relationships, talk through misunderstandings, and support one another. This month, you'll be stronger (and smarter!) together than you are on your own. Then everything kicks up a notch when Mars retrograde ends on the 23rd: time to start chasing those big dreams!

Moon Cycles

On the 12th, the Leo Full Moon could activate your deepest insecurities: you *want* attention and love, but you're scared to let people see the real you! Carving out some alone time *now* to care for yourself will help you shine brighter in the long run.

Then on the 27th, the Pisces New Moon is a great time to begin a new relationship. If you've been hesitant to let your guard down and open up to someone in your life, this could be your moment to finally go for it.

Power Days

If you're open and direct about your feelings on the 1st, it's likely to lead to good (though potentially unexpected!) outcomes. The 6th is a lucky day for you, especially in career matters: projects you start now should go incredibly well. The 23rd is a great day to ask a friend for a big favor.

Days to Watch For

On the 7th, you'll probably see the worst in everyone, including yourself: give people (especially your partner) the benefit of the doubt. Expect some relationship tension on the 14th, but it should pass soon, so don't read too much into it. It's easy to accidentally hurt feelings on the 25th: if you have to give negative feedback, do it gently.

March

This month is defined by two retrogrades: Venus retrograde begins on the 1st, and Mercury retrograde starts on the 15th.

Expect plenty of surprises this month—some inconvenient maybe, but some good! Sometimes when your original plans are disrupted, *better* plans can emerge. This retrograde also means that Venus moves back into Pisces, giving you a second chance to work out any relationship issues that arose last month (or to seize the moment to ask someone out, if you missed your chance in February!).

Moon Cycles

Eclipse season is here! On the 14th, the lunar eclipse in Virgo should be especially potent for you. This is your moment to assert yourself, to take up space, to seize control of your own destiny. If you've forgotten how powerful you truly are, let this eclipse remind you.

Then on the 29th, the solar eclipse in Aries invites you to turn over a new leaf. (Even if you aren't ready for transformation, it might come knocking on your door anyway!) Especially if you've felt out of control with your finances, this is a perfect opportunity for a reset.

Power Days

Life-changing encounters are possible on the 5th: if you've been longing to connect on a deeper level, this is your moment. You'll feel highly energized on the 7th: it's a good day for working, but an even better one for getting involved in your community. If you've felt overlooked or pushed around, stand up for yourself on the 28th!

Days to Watch For

It could be easy to get the wrong impression of potential partners on the 2nd: don't put your crush on a pedestal! Relationships with colleagues are likely to be tense and frustrating on the 6th, but any trouble should blow over soon. You may be irritable on the 13th: don't take your bad mood out on the people you care about.

April

Mercury and Venus retrograde both end this month (Mercury on the 7th, Venus on the 12th), and after that, no planets are retrograde for the rest of the month. Any miscommunications and disruptions you experienced in March should ease off now. Mercury and Venus both move into Aries this month (on the 16th and 30th, respectively). A financial windfall may come your way: be smart about how you spend it! Relationships may get more emotionally intense right now. Even if you've kept things relatively light so far, they could get serious fast.

Moon Cycles

The Libra Full Moon on the 12th might highlight issues related to money and values: maybe finances aren't divided equitably in a relationship, or maybe you and someone you love are in conflict because of your different values. Make the most of this opportunity to rebalance things.

On the 27th, the New Moon in Taurus activates your adventurous side. Suddenly you want to visit beautiful new cities, taste new foods, and experience all that the world has to offer. This is a great time for planning trips and luxurious new experiences.

Power Days

Generosity pays off on the 2nd: treat others (even rivals!) right, and your good deeds will come back to you. Be assertive on the 6th! Ask for what you want, and you're likely to get it. If you step outside your usual routines on the 8th, you're likely to meet somebody thrilling and new.

Days to Watch For

Dates (especially first dates) aren't likely to go well on the 3rd, so pick another day if you can. Reason and emotion are in conflict on the 10th: be patient with yourself as you sort through your true desires. The honeymoon phase in any relationship is likely to end on the 24th: be ready to deal with the tough realities.

May

Your career takes center stage when the Sun and Mercury enter Gemini this month (the Sun on the 20th, Mercury on the 25th). If you've been working hard but feeling overlooked, that should change now. Your steady contributions haven't gone unnoticed after all. Don't hesitate to remind your boss or colleagues of all that you've accomplished, and don't be shy about telling others about your big, long-term goals. People *want* to help you advance in your career—but they can't do that if they don't know what you're aiming for!

Moon Cycles

Under the Scorpio Full Moon on the 12th, expect to be busy. It may feel like everyone in your life is demanding to have big, important conversations with you *right now*. Lean into the intensity: it'll be rewarding and surprisingly refreshing!

On the 26th, the New Moon in Gemini creates the perfect conditions to rethink your professional goals. Where do you want to be a year from now? How do you want others to see you? Intentions you set today will take you far.

Power Days

The 6th is one of those days when everything just seems to go your way. Enjoy it! On the 13th, you could meet someone who's going to be an important person in your life. The 24th is an excellent time for presentations and job interviews—or really in any part of your life where you want to make a strong first impression.

Days to Watch For

Don't take negative feelings *too* seriously on the 5th: you're ultrasensitive right now and might be reading too much into things. Be mindful of your words on the 7th—it's easy to speak carelessly and rub others the wrong way right now. Don't be self-deprecating at work on the 15th, or your boss might just believe you.

June

This is a big social month for you, with Mercury, Jupiter, and the Sun all moving into Cancer and your solar eleventh house of groups and community (on the 8th, 9th, and 20th, respectively). Make a point of spending time with friends, participating in group activities, and getting involved in the community: it'll bring insight, meaning, and luck into your life right now! Mars also enters Virgo on the 17th, which means that this month is likely to be *busy*. It's a great time to make strides toward your goals; just be careful not to trample others along the way.

Moon Cycles

On the 11th, the Full Moon in Sagittarius calls your attention to issues in your home life. If your living space would benefit from repairs or a refresh, now's the time to take action! Devote extra attention to your relationships with the people you live with.

Then on the 25th, the New Moon in Cancer is a great time to join a new cause or group. If you've been feeling a little isolated or lonely lately, commit to connecting with people. Volunteering and helping others is one of the best ways to do this.

Power Days

You can make huge progress at work on the 8th: from leading people to sharing your ideas to negotiating, you can do it all today. The 26th should be a high-energy day for you—and if you team up with others, you'll be unstoppable. The 29th is a great day for taking risks: have faith in yourself!

Days to Watch For

Unrealistic expectations (of yourself *and* others) can cause problems on the 2nd. If conflict arises on the 3rd, don't bury your head in the sand: open communication (even when it's hard) will lead to stronger relationships. On the 20th, you may need a reminder that it isn't your job to solve everyone else's problems.

July

Three planets station retrograde this month: Neptune, Saturn, and Mercury. During this Mercury retrograde, which lasts from the 18th to August 11th, you're less likely to experience external mishaps and more likely to run up against inner confusion. But if you use this time to slow down and reflect, you may reach major insights. Venus and Uranus both move into Gemini this month, on the 4th and 7th, respectively. Venus's influence should make you popular and successful at work, but expect Uranus to bring some career surprises (possibly very good ones!) your way, too.

Moon Cycles

The Capricorn Full Moon on the 10th is an invitation for you to have some fun! No matter what obligations are on your plate right now, be sure to carve out some time for self-expression, creativity, and play: all of this is just as necessary as hard work!

Then on the 24th, the Leo New Moon may have you feeling exhausted. You've been doing a *lot* lately and experiencing major growth (probably more than you even realize). Under this Moon, treat yourself to some peace and quiet.

Power Days

The 1st is a great day for romance—relationships might not be that deep right now, but they will be thrilling! On the 4th, work collaboratively with others: remember that you don't have to take on the world all by yourself! Alone time on the 20th will help you reconnect with your unique ideas, desires, and purpose in life.

Days to Watch For

Long-simmering issues with a family member or roommate may boil over on the 7th: try not to do further damage as you hash things out. You may make unwise romantic choices on the 23rd: sometimes that's fun, but just be careful! Take care not to jump to conclusions on the 26th, or you may land yourself in an embarrassing situation.

August

Mars leaves Virgo and enters Libra on the 6th. This could be a great time for financial moves on your part, but try to keep a balanced mindset and don't rush into anything! You can breathe a sigh of relief when Mercury retrograde ends on the 11th: all the inner confusion of the past month should finally resolve into clarity. Finally—and most importantly for you—the Sun enters Virgo on the 22nd! This is your time to shine. You spend so much time and energy helping others: take this time to think about what *you* want and need.

Moon Cycles

On the 9th, the Aquarius Full Moon is a good time for quitting any routines that just don't work for you anymore. Remember that you can't keep adding new activities and commitments to your plate. In order to make room for the new, you have to release the old!

Then on the 23rd, the New Moon in Virgo offers a powerful opportunity to start fresh. If you don't like where your life is going—or if you simply want *more* for yourself—then now is your moment. Right now, anything's possible if you believe in yourself.

Power Days

The 3rd is a good day for discussing memories with someone close to you: you can learn a lot by delving into your past. You're likely to be lucky in love on the 10th, so don't underestimate your own attractiveness! The 22nd is one of the best days of the year for new beginnings: here's your chance to reinvent yourself.

Days to Watch For

It's easy to feel defensive—especially with the people you live with—on the 5th. Try to keep an even keel! It's important to find an outlet for your emotions and energies on the 24th: if you try to bottle things up, you just might explode. People may get on your nerves on the 30th, so try to be patient (or just walk away!).

September

Mercury joins the Sun in Virgo on the 2nd, and Venus follows on the 19th. With all these planets lined up in your sign, this should be a powerful time for you, and a reminder that you can shine bright, just as you are. No need to try to change yourself to make others happy: you'll be most popular and successful right now simply by being *you*. The Sun moves into Libra on the 22nd. This is a great time for bringing beauty into your life. Treat yourself!

Moon Cycles

The second eclipse season of the year is here! First up is the Pisces lunar eclipse on the 7th. There's a strong likelihood of conflict or shake-ups in close relationships, but any change that happens now is probably necessary, and good for you in the long run.

Then on the 21st, the solar eclipse in Virgo is the year's second eclipse to occur in your sign. This could provide the push you've needed to have faith in yourself and dream big. Your life belongs to *you*, and it's up to you to make the most of it.

Power Days

Tell someone you love (romantically *or* platonically) how you feel on the 11th: it's an ideal day for expressing emotion and connecting. The 12th should be an incredibly lucky day for you:

whatever you put your mind to now is likely to turn out well. The 24th is a lovely day for a get-together or dinner party.

Days to Watch For

The 7th is not the day for challenging or emotionally sensitive conversations: wait a day or two if possible. Tensions between your professional life and personal life might arise on the 14th, so be prepared to prioritize. You may feel bored by your life on the 20th: it's good to shake up your routines, but don't do anything *too* drastic.

October

Venus enters Libra on the 13th. This may be a time of exciting financial opportunities for you, like a promotion or a raise, but the more important thing is to focus on what *you* really value. If you're going to take a new job or start dating someone new, do so because it's the right choice for *you*—not because you think it'll impress somebody else. Mercury enters Sagittarius on the 29th: this is an ideal time to sort out issues related to your house or family life.

Moon Cycles

If you've been dealing with a stressful financial situation for a while—especially related to debt, divorce, or an inheritance—

there's a good chance you can finally put it to bed and start fresh under the Aries Full Moon on the 6th.

On the 21st, the Libra New Moon invites you to focus on enjoying the world around you: What gives you pleasure? Where do you find beauty? Especially if you've been focused on practical matters lately, take a moment to do something that brings you joy today.

Power Days

The 8th is a lovely day for socializing—the bigger the group, the better (and the more likely you'll be to find a special connection). Listen to your instincts on the 9th: your subconscious knows things your rational mind doesn't yet. Take the lead on the 17th: you won't get what you want if you wait around for an invitation.

Days to Watch For

You'll probably feel unmotivated on the 11th: avoid scheduling important events (even fun ones!) for today if you can. On the 16th, be prepared for dramatic mood swings. Don't take action based on your emotions now, because they could change at any moment. You're likely to feel insecure on the 26th: if you need reassurance from your partner, *ask*.

November

The third and final Mercury retrograde of the year is here, lasting from the 9th to the 29th. As always, slow down, show yourself and others lots of grace, and double-check your work! Saturn retrograde ends on the 27th, and could lead to a reckoning with someone close to you, like a partner or close friend. Remind yourself that the people in your life should support you, not hold you back. When Venus enters Sagittarius on the 30th, schedule some nice quiet time at home. It'll feel extra rejuvenating now.

Moon Cycles

The Taurus Full Moon on the 5th marks a moment when you may have to step outside your comfort zone—no matter how scary it feels. Life can't stay the same forever. If you take a leap of faith now, it may change your life for the better.

Your social instincts will be extra sharp under the New Moon in Scorpio on the 20th. It's a good time for filling up your calendar, connecting with new people, and having conversations about topics that matter deeply to you. Even small interactions have the potential to be incredibly meaningful today.

Power Days

On the 2nd, you'll have the clarity and courage you need to make important decisions (but still ask for support if you need it!). The 14th is a good day for explaining your perspective and getting others—from colleagues to neighbors—on your side. The 29th is a good day for giving and receiving emotional support, so don't be scared to ask.

Days to Watch For

Conflict is likely on the 4th, especially if you've let resentment build up. Emotion could cloud your judgment on the 8th, so best not to make any major decisions today. Tensions could rise to the surface of your relationships on the 28th, but if you can both communicate honestly about how you're feeling, things will work out fine.

December

December might just be one of the most romantic months of the year for you! While the first half of the month is focused on Sagittarius (and your solar fourth house of home and family), the planets begin moving into Capricorn (and your solar fifth house of romance, creativity, and pleasure) midway through: Mars on the 15th, the Sun on the 21st, and Venus on the 24th. You don't always give yourself permission to simply enjoy your life, but that's the best possible thing you can do right now.

Moon Cycles

Like it or not, the Gemini Full Moon on the 4th makes you feel like the center of attention! This might not feel totally comfortable, but it should be rewarding. There's a strong likelihood that you'll get some lovely public recognition for all your hard work.

Under the Sagittarius New Moon on the 19th, the best thing you can do is listen to your gut. If you're facing a big decision right now, it's good to ask for advice—but ultimately your own instincts will provide the best road map forward.

Power Days

The 7th is a good day for looking to the future, planning ahead, and making lasting commitments (in both your work life *and* your personal life). Express yourself on the 26th: creativity will open new doors right now. On the 31st, your relationships with others can be transformed for the better through deep, vulnerable conversations.

Days to Watch For

Trying to start ambitious new projects on the 8th will probably lead to frustration; instead, keep working on the ones that are already in the pipeline. If you face setbacks on the 16th, don't give up: perseverance is what's needed now. It's easy to feel down on yourself on the 20th, so surround yourself with people who encourage you.

Libra

The Scales
September 22 to October 22

Element: Air
Ruling planet: Venus
Keyword: Thoughtful
Key phrase: I balance

Gemstone: Opal
Power stones: Tourmaline, blue lace agate
Color: Pink
Flower: Rose

All about Libra

Strengths and Gifts

The Sun enters Libra, symbolized by the scales, with the autumnal equinox. Libra is an intelligent and sophisticated air sign, and it's ruled by Venus, the planet of beauty. Just as the equinox is the moment when day and night are perfectly balanced, you, Libra, are motivated by a desire for fairness, harmony, and balance.

Your abiding interest in fairness makes you a kind and deeply likable person. More than any other sign, Libras try to approach the world with an open mind and without bias. In part, this is because Libra is an air sign, able to observe people and situations clearly and rationally, without letting emotions color your judgment. (This isn't to say that you don't *have* deep emotions, of course—only that you strive to give everyone a fair shake, regardless of any first impressions or prior experiences.)

You're something of a social butterfly, popular in many different social groups. When you throw a party (you're probably *great* at entertaining!), people from many different circles are likely to show up, and you see to it that *everyone* has a wonderful time. You're able to see the best in most people you encounter, and in turn, they also see the best in *you*.

Your commitment to fairness and balance extends to decision-making, too. While others seem to make decisions at the speed of light, you're much more deliberate. You examine situations from every angle, do your best to put yourself in others' shoes, and think through all the pros and cons. You rarely make rash or ill-informed choices—but this means that it may take you a long time to make up your mind! Others may sometimes perceive this thoroughness as indecisiveness, but the fact is that once you finally *do* make a choice, it's almost always one you can stand by.

Finally, no description of Libra would be complete without mentioning your pitch-perfect sense of aesthetics. Thanks to your ruling planet, Venus, and your innate desire for harmony, you've got an excellent eye for design: when it comes to choosing colors, pulling outfits together, or arranging furniture, you're a natural! This doesn't mean you're obsessed with fashion or clothes—many Libras couldn't care less—only that you bring a touch of elegance and style with you in whatever you do.

Friendship and Love

With Venus as your ruling planet, love—and not only the romantic kind!—comes naturally to you. You're keenly attuned to social dynamics, gifted at setting people at ease, and able to bring out the best in friends and partners alike. You treat the people in your life with fairness and respect, and your friends know they can count on you. Even more than that, with your charm and grace, you're simply delightful to be around!

In group settings, you're often the peacemaker, the one who makes sure everyone's happy. If someone is feeling a bit left out, you'll make a point of including them in the conversation. If two of your friends aren't getting along, you'll help to smooth things out. In one-on-one relationships, you tend to be kind and accommodating. If your partner has a plan for your upcoming vacation, or your date has strong preferences about where to go for dinner, then by all means, let them take the lead! You aren't fussy or demanding—and in fact, when it comes to unimportant matters, you're probably happier *not* having to make the decision.

While some people seem drawn toward conflict and find peaceful relationships boring, you're probably the opposite. You find big, dramatic ups and downs in your relationships stressful, not thrilling—you prefer steady, balanced harmony. When clashes inevitably arise—as they do in all relationships!—you're good at working things out calmly and thoughtfully.

The trouble is that sometimes you're a bit too conflict-avoidant. Disagreements with loved ones may not be pleasant, but they're necessary—even healthy! When you're too quick to paper over any discomfort, or when you ignore your own feelings for the sake of peace in the relationship, that doesn't benefit either one of you in the long run. In order to build true, lasting intimacy, it's important to acknowledge disagreements, to be honest about frustrations and insecurities, and to be honest— with the other person and yourself—about what *you* need. This may feel, at first, like you're being selfish or demanding, but ultimately it'll make your relationships stronger.

Work and Money

You're a fantastic coworker, Libra: you understand the value of good working relationships, and you understand that these relationships don't happen on their own, but take effort and commitment. You'd make an excellent manager in just about any field; you're great at managing team dynamics, and you'd make sure that everyone is treated fairly. Libras also shine in fields where they can put their negotiation skills into practice: from local politics to big law firms, you know how to be persuasive and get other people on your side. And, of course, you're also likely to excel in work that involves style, beauty, or design, from hairdressing to photography to architecture.

When it comes to finances, your approach is defined by one word: *balance*. As much as you love beautiful things (and can be tempted to spend big!), keeping a balanced budget is important enough that you're unlikely ever to go *too* nuts. Sometimes, though, you end up accepting terms that are disadvantageous for you (say, a lower salary than you deserve or an unfair split of expenses with a roommate) in order to accommodate somebody else. Advocate for yourself!

Struggles and Growth

Sometimes your desire to be diplomatic prevents you from taking a stand. You let other people's rudeness slide because you want to give them the benefit of the doubt, or you hesitate to voice your opinion because you worry it'll rub someone the wrong way. Just because you're likable by nature, that doesn't mean it's your duty to be liked by *everyone*—that's impossible! Try not to worry so much about how you're coming across to others. The truth is that when you're honest and true to yourself, you'll attract the right people to you.

Your thoughtful, careful decision-making process is a tremendously valuable asset, but every so often, your desire to have
all the information before moving forward can hold you back.
Sometimes there's no way to get all the details or to see a problem from every possible angle—but if you trust your gut and
take a leap of faith, things will work out just right.

Journaling Page

Think about your goals for 2025. Which of your Libra
gifts—charm, tact, smarts, style—will you call on to help you
achieve them? Which elements of the Libra personality do
you want to lean into this year?

The Year Ahead for Libra

The Eclipses

Eclipses happen every year, and by paying attention to them, you can get a good sense of the main plot points of the months ahead. They mark the major beginnings, endings, and twists in the story of your year (although, depending on what's in your personal birth chart, you'll feel some eclipses more intensely than others!). The year 2025 has four eclipses: lunar eclipses in Virgo and Pisces and solar eclipses in Aries and Virgo.

The first of these is the Virgo lunar eclipse on March 14th. Today, whatever's been simmering beneath the surface—whether it's a feeling you've been trying to downplay or a worry you've wanted to ignore—is likely to rise up and demand that you deal with it. Devote some energy to whatever comes up today; no more avoiding it.

Later in the month, an Aries solar eclipse on March 29th brings a new beginning in the realm of close relationships. This could mean that you'll begin to date someone new, or it could mean that you and an existing partner are entering into a new phase. You might not be ready for the change this eclipse brings, but it's probably going to be just what you needed.

Then on September 7th, a Pisces lunar eclipse is an ideal moment to change up your routines. (Even if you don't think you *want* to change things, the universe might make it unavoidable!)

It's easy to get stuck in a rut in your daily life: this is your chance to bring your daily habits in line with your higher self.

Finally, there's another eclipse in Virgo on September 21st—this time, a solar eclipse. While it might be tempting to rush around, start new projects, and fill your calendar with activities, the best thing to do right now is rest and recharge.

The Big Picture

After checking in on the eclipses, you can find more clues about your year ahead by looking to the outer planets of Jupiter, Saturn, Uranus, Neptune, and Pluto. These planets, which move slowly through the zodiac and stay in the same sign for months or even years at a time, can give you a good sense of the big-picture story of 2025.

Let's start with **Jupiter**, planet of growth and luck. It begins the year in Gemini and your solar ninth house of travel and learning, which makes this an *excellent* time for big trips (especially to other countries) and applying to or enrolling in educational programs. If you've been dreaming of taking that dream trip, consider booking it for the first half of 2025! On June 9th, Jupiter moves into Cancer, where it'll stay for the rest of the year. At this point, the focus shifts to your career: hard work, professional networking, and applying for your dream job (even if you're worried you're underqualified) are especially likely to pay off now.

Next up is **Saturn**, planet of structure, discipline, and hard work. Saturn starts 2025 in Pisces, moves into Aries on May 24th, and returns to Pisces on September 1st. While it's in Pisces, there's a chance you'll feel overwhelmed by the responsibilities of daily life: there are so many details to attend to! But while it may be tempting to let things slide—or even give up— the more attention you pay to the small stuff now, the happier you'll be later on. When Saturn is in Aries, it's a good time to invest in relationships, whether that means with a partner, a best friend, or even a coworker. It's worthwhile to find common ground, even (or especially) with people who are very different from you.

Neptune, planet of fantasy and confusion, also splits its time between Pisces and Aries this year, starting off in Pisces, moving into Aries on March 30th, and returning to Pisces on October 22nd. While Neptune is in Pisces, it's easy to feel like kind of a hypochondriac or even to fall for weird wellness scams. When it comes to health matters, be extra sure to get advice from someone trustworthy. Then when Neptune enters Aries, be extra careful that you're not rushing into new relationships, whether personal or professional. It's easy to be taken in by big promises or overlook red flags right now.

Uranus, planet of progress and unpredictability, starts out in Taurus, moves into Gemini from July 7th through November

7th, then returns to Taurus (before moving into Gemini for the long haul in early 2026). In the time since Uranus first entered Taurus in 2018, you've probably felt your life shaken by big ups and downs, financial windfalls and setbacks, or relationship beginnings and endings. This story is drawing to a close now—you've almost made it! Once Uranus enters Gemini, expect a major mindset shift: you've learned so much, and you're seeing the world (and your life) through new eyes now.

Last but not least, intense and mystical **Pluto** continues its yearslong journey through Aquarius, where it'll be until 2043. This year, let Pluto empower you in expressing yourself. Whether through writing, art, or simply conversation, this is an ideal time to open up and be honest, even if you're worried your feelings or opinions won't make you popular.

Your Ruling Planet

Your ruling planet, Libra, is Venus: planet of love, beauty, and values. Lucky you! This is where your likability and eye for beauty come from. But because of your connection with the planet of love, it means that Venus retrograde is a key event for you to keep an eye on. In 2025, Venus stations retrograde in Aries on March 1st, moves backward into Pisces on March 27th, and then starts moving forward again on April 12th. While Venus moves backward through Aries and your solar seventh house of partnership, there's a good chance your close relationships will feel a bit out of whack. (Outside of Venus retrograde, February 1—when Venus aligns with confusing Neptune—is also a day to avoid making important relationship decisions.) While Venus is retrograde in Pisces, there's a chance you may suddenly lose confidence in your body or appearance. Don't take action until the retrograde is over, or you likely won't be satisfied with the results!

January

The year 2025 kicks off with three retrograde planets: Mars, Jupiter, and Uranus. Jupiter and Uranus retrograde shouldn't be too personally disruptive for you, but with Mars retrograde in Leo, there's a good chance you'll experience some conflict in your friend group. Try not to fan the flames by taking sides right now. Mars moves backward into Cancer on the 6th. When it does, avoid the temptation to take bold action in your career. (In other words, if you've been thinking about dramatically quitting your job, wait until Mars retrograde ends next month!)

Moon Cycles

The year begins with a Full Moon in Cancer on January 13th. You'll probably feel the pressure to perform right now—all eyes are on you, especially at work. You've got so much to offer, and this is your moment to shine.

Then on the 29th, the Aquarius New Moon should be an especially fun and lovely one for you. It's possible that you'll suddenly see a friend in a more romantic light. The world feels full of possibilities right now, so give yourself permission to dream big!

Power Days

Be assertive on the 5th: you'll never get what you want by waiting around forever! The 12th is a good day for making big decisions (especially about work issues): your instincts are on point. You're likely to experience a lucky break that leads to long-term positive change on the 19th.

Days to Watch For

Be prepared for some tension involving your partner, family, or roommates on the 6th: don't ignore the problem or it'll only get worse! Old insecurities are likely to pop up on the 8th—don't let the past ruin a good thing in the present. Conflict at work is likely on the 15th: respond with assertiveness, *not* passive-aggression.

February

On the 4th, Venus moves into Aries, making this one of the best months of the year for you to start a new relationship or strengthen an existing one. Don't wait around for someone else to take the lead. The more assertive (not aggressive!) you are, the more luck you're likely to have—and the more honest and direct you are about what you want, the better. Mars retrograde ends on the 23rd, which means that the time for bold or even potentially risky career moves is now.

Moon Cycles

Under the Leo Full Moon on the 12th, be ready for a bit of drama in your social circle—maybe even involving you! People's needs and expectations clash sometimes, but if you're honest and kind (and don't get defensive), it'll all turn out fine.

Then on the 27th, the New Moon in Pisces is an ideal time to reflect on your routines. Are your daily habits supporting your higher self? Are they bringing you closer to the person you want to be? If not, now's your moment to make a change.

Power Days

Romance gets extra intense on the 7th. Whether you're in a relationship or just meeting someone new, expect deep conversations and steamy encounters. Advocate for yourself on the 9th! It's an especially good day to negotiate a raise. Things are likely to go your way on the 17th, and it's a great day for scheduling social activities.

Days to Watch For

Everyone is likely to be cranky on the 3rd: treat people (including yourself!) with a bit of extra gentleness. The 15th probably isn't the best day for dating: relationships are likely to feel off-balance right now. On the 24th, you may get the sense that others are picking on you: don't be scared to stand up for yourself.

March

Venus retrograde begins on the 1st, making March (and the first half of April) a less than ideal time for starting relationships.

(It's not impossible, of course, just don't rush into anything!) It's also a good idea to avoid making any big aesthetic changes, from getting a dramatic haircut to painting your bedroom. Mercury retrograde also starts on the 15th and lasts until April 7th. Especially from the 15th to the 29th, negotiations of all kinds— whether you're discussing a business agreement, your salary, a legal matter, or something else—are likely to be difficult, so consider rescheduling if you can.

Moon Cycles

Eclipse season is here! On the 14th, the lunar eclipse in Virgo is likely to illuminate some major emotional truths for you. If you've been trying to ignore a feeling in your gut, that's not going to be possible anymore. Be honest with yourself.

Then on the 29th, the Aries solar eclipse opens the door to a new phase of a relationship. You could turn over a new leaf with a partner, come to a new understanding with a longtime friend, or even find yourself in a brand-new whirlwind romance.

Power Days

The 1st is an ideal day to begin a new relationship (or even rekindle an old one). If you keep your eyes and ears open on the 5th, you're likely to learn valuable information (or just hear juicy gossip!). Make a point of spending time with friends on the 10th: a little socializing is just what you need today.

Days to Watch For

It's easy to accidentally hurt someone you care about on the 2nd: don't be too proud to apologize! The smallest things could set off an argument on the 15th, but a little grace and understanding will go a long way. You're not likely to feel your best on the 16th, so avoid scheduling important events today if possible.

April

Both of last month's retrogrades end in April! Mercury stations direct on the 7th, followed by Venus on the 12th. (After this, *no* planets are retrograde through the end of the month, making this a great opportunity to take big steps forward and make progress toward your goals.) Mercury moves into Aries on the 16th, and Venus returns to Aries on the 30th. With both of these important planets in your solar seventh house of relationships, it's a great time to focus on your connections with the people closest to you.

Moon Cycles

On the 12th, the Libra Full Moon is your invitation to be fully, unapologetically *you*. Today, your job is to stop apologizing or feeling guilty for who you are. It's great to be accommodating of others, but *your* needs matter, too, and it's up to you to remember that.

Then on the 27th, the New Moon in Taurus makes it possible to change your life in unexpected ways. If you dig deep into your desires right now, you'll find surprising (but effective!) ways to get what you want.

Power Days

From small favors to a big promotion, the 5th is a great day to ask for what you want: things are likely to go your way. Spend time with friends or go on a date on the 6th. Your intuition is strong on the 12th—if you get a feeling about something or someone, trust it!

Days to Watch For

You might experience some tension between your work and your personal life on the 4th, and you'll have to prioritize. It's easy to take things *way* too personally on the 10th: don't assume the worst of other people. Your judgment is likely to be clouded on the 25th, so avoid making important decisions today.

May

The Sun and Mercury both move into Gemini this month (the Sun on the 20th, Mercury on the 25th). One of the best things you can do for yourself now is broaden your horizons, whether that means trying a new activity, traveling to a new city (or even country!), or attending a lecture. When Saturn moves into Aries on the 24th, you'll be faced with questions about the long-term viability of your close relationships. Are you ready to commit? If not, what needs to change?

Moon Cycles

On the 12th, the Full Moon in Scorpio may illuminate the places in your life where you feel like something important is missing. You deserve to feel good about your life, so if something isn't quite measuring up, don't be scared to make a change.

On the 26th, a New Moon in Gemini might make you a bit restless and ready to take on new challenges. Let yourself dream big, but don't rush into any commitments or definite plans (unless you're *sure* about them!)—instead, luxuriate in the sense of possibility.

Power Days

Open up about your feelings on the 9th (especially if something's been weighing on you): it'll lead to closer relationships. The likelihood for exciting chance encounters, even a meet-cute, is high on the 17th, so put yourself out there. Your charm is amplified on the 23rd: make the most of it!

Days to Watch For

You're likely to put new people on a pedestal on the 1st: be careful not to let your guard down too quickly! On the 8th, your heart's probably extra sensitive, so avoid putting yourself into difficult or dramatic situations as much as possible. You may feel sad or isolated on the 28th: plan to take good care of yourself.

June

Mercury, Jupiter, and the Sun all move into Cancer this month (on the 8th, 9th, and 20th, respectively), making this a big career month for you. If you've been working toward a particular milestone or hoping for an accolade or a promotion, there's a good chance it'll happen now. On the other hand, if you've felt a bit stagnant or directionless, look at this as your opportunity to change that. It's a great time for rediscovering your ambition and focus, making a plan, and beginning to move toward your professional goals.

Moon Cycles

The Full Moon in Sagittarius on the 11th is likely to be an exceptionally busy time for you! Your schedule is bursting and your brain is firing on all cylinders. There's probably no real way around this, so schedule some downtime in the next few days if you can.

On the 25th, the New Moon in Cancer is an ideal day for setting fresh intentions, especially those related to your work life, career, or reputation. What do you want to achieve? How do you want to be remembered? What can you start doing *now* to get there?

Power Days

You're charming and delightful on the 5th: flirt, socialize, go out to a party! The 24th is likely to be an amazing career day for you: this is a truly ideal time to start a new job or project. On the 25th, don't wait for good luck to come to you—be assertive!

Days to Watch For

You may feel a bit gloomy on the 4th, so be careful not to let a momentary bad mood ruin an otherwise good relationship. The 15th could bring a major turning point: change won't be easy now, but it will be worth it. You may face a career hurdle on the 22nd: persevere and keep working hard, and you'll get through this.

July

Three retrogrades start this month: Neptune on the 4th, Saturn on the 13th, and Mercury on the 18th. Of these three, Mercury's the one you're most likely to notice in your daily life. In particular, watch out for drama and misunderstandings in your friend group (or in any other groups, from clubs to classes, that you're part of). Venus and Uranus both move into Gemini this month (on the 4th and 7th, respectively): you might get unexpected opportunities to travel or fall in love with someone totally outside your usual type. Either way, go for it!

Moon Cycles

There's a good chance you'll experience a bit of drama with family or roommates under the Capricorn Full Moon on the 10th. The best thing to do is simply lean into it. Dealing with whatever pops up now will put you in a *much* better place ultimately.

Under the Leo New Moon on the 24th, there's a strong possibility that you'll meet someone who ends up being important in your life—whether professionally, personally, or even romantically. A casual encounter could bloom into something significant, so put yourself out there and see what happens.

Power Days

The 5th is likely to bring good financial news, like a raise, a windfall, or a deal finally going through. On the 11th, don't take on hard projects alone: working closely with someone you trust will take you *much* further. Help others in your community on the 24th, and you're likely to be rewarded for it, too.

Days to Watch For

Things probably seem *much* worse than they really are on the 1st, so wait a day or two before you take any drastic measures. Overconfidence may cause problems on the 2nd: try to stay humble! Mix-ups and miscommunications are likely on the 9th, so make an extra effort to understand the people you care about.

August

Mars moves into Libra on the 6th! (This is the first time all year that a planet is entering your home sign. It's about time!) This makes it a great time for you to assert yourself, stand up for your rights, and fight back if someone is treating you poorly. The key is to do so without trampling all over anyone else's feelings. Mercury retrograde ends on the 11th: if you got tangled up in any dramas during this time or accidentally hurt a friend's feelings, you have a chance now to make things right.

Moon Cycles

On the 9th, the Full Moon in Aquarius wants you to express yourself! If you have a big pie-in-the-sky dream that you've been keeping to yourself, or a brilliant idea that you're worried is too "out there," this is the perfect time to share it.

Then under the Virgo New Moon on the 23rd, it's important to get some rest. If possible, carve out some time to relax by yourself. Life's been busy lately, and you need some peace and quiet to process it all and figure out what's next.

Power Days

The 8th is a great day for changing up old routines (just be careful not to mess things up for people you care about!). Your ambitious side is activated on the 10th: dream *big* and the universe will help you out. The 11th is a seriously romantic day. If you're single, there's a good chance you'll meet someone through work today.

Days to Watch For

You might feel a bit shy or insecure on the 1st, so try to spend time with the friends who make you feel the best about yourself. You might feel split between your partner and your family on the 5th—don't feel forced to take sides! The 25th may feel a bit chaotic, but any problems that arise today will probably be temporary.

September

For roughly the first half of this month, while the Sun and Mercury are in Virgo, you may find yourself in an especially reflective mood. Do yourself a favor and make the most of this opportunity to rest and recharge. Then on the 18th, Mercury moves into Libra, followed by the Sun on the 22nd. This is your chance to step into your power! You should feel confident and energized right now. You know who you are and what you want, and you're ready to take on the world.

Moon Cycles

It's eclipse season again! It's hard to break bad habits. If you've been struggling to make a change (particularly related to your health or your daily routines), the universe might give you a little push under the Pisces lunar eclipse on the 7th.

Then under the solar eclipse in Virgo on the 21st, you get a chance to start fresh. You've made mistakes in the past (who hasn't!), but you've grown from it. Don't beat yourself up about what's done; just take the lessons you've learned and move forward from here.

Power Days

The 5th is a perfect day for asking someone out—or for making any kind of bold, exciting suggestion. Expand your horizons on the 21st by trying something new or spending time with someone outside your usual circle. Take a risk or two on the 23rd: it's likely to pay off in a big way.

Days to Watch For

You might be tempted to act recklessly on the 4th—don't do it! Careful planning will make everything go better. Think before you speak on the 9th, or you may end up saying something you regret. Family or roommates might get on your nerves in a big way on the 29th, but try to be kind.

October

On the 6th, Mercury leaves Libra and enters Scorpio, where it'll stay until the 29th. The Sun joins it in Scorpio on the 22nd. This means that for much of the month, but especially the period between the 22nd and 29th, money will become a focus. Spend some time digging into your financial affairs: if things aren't as they should be, now's a good opportunity to make it right. Also, Venus enters Libra on the 13th! You're likely at your most charming and popular right now, so make the most of it.

Moon Cycles

On the 6th, a Full Moon in Aries could set off a conflict with somebody close to you. This isn't a bad thing—think of it as an opportunity for both of you to be honest so that you can clear the air. Ultimately, it could even bring you closer.

Then on the 21st, the New Moon in Libra is one of the best days of the year for you to turn over a new leaf. If you've been wanting to make a change—new haircut, new relationship, or whole new outlook on life—this could be the day.

Power Days

The 2nd is likely to be one of those days where it feels like you just can't lose, so have fun and make the most of it! Expect the unexpected on the 14th—in a good way! Step outside your comfort zone and you'll discover a new side of yourself. On the 19th, you should have rewarding encounters with new people.

Days to Watch For

Your instincts about other people—even those closest to you—
might be a bit muddled on the 6th. It's easy to overcommit (both
professionally and socially) on the 16th: think before you say yes
to anything! Be careful not to ignore your own limits or boundaries on the 21st: it's easy to go overboard right now.

November

The third and final Mercury retrograde happens this month,
beginning on the 9th in Sagittarius, moving backward into
Scorpio on the 18th, and ending on the 29th. During this retrograde, especially between the 9th and 18th, it's likely you'll
experience scheduling issues (particularly relating to travel)
and time zone snafus. You're at risk of double-booking yourself—or even missing appointments altogether. Just do your
best, and try to be understanding with others if they're late or
disorganized. You'll probably need them to cut *you* some slack
at some point, too.

Moon Cycles

On the 5th, the Full Moon in Taurus might activate money
matters (and may even signal an unexpected windfall!). Don't
be scared to ask for financial help today if you need it—or, more
likely, to lend a hand to others if you're in a position to do so.

Under the Scorpio New Moon on the 20th, think about what you really value in life. Are you devoting enough time to the things that make *you* happy, or are you spending all your time taking care of others? It isn't too late to make a change.

Power Days

Pay attention to your intuition on the 10th, even if it doesn't seem logical. You're likely to have a stroke of good luck—especially relating to work or money—on the 16th. The 26th is a great day for love, whether you're looking to meet someone new, rekindle an old spark, or just keep a good thing going.

Days to Watch For

You'll likely feel unmotivated on the 2nd, so try to avoid scheduling important obligations for today. Your expectations may clash with your partner's on the 4th: honesty and openness will go a long way toward fixing things. On the 17th, you may get the wrong read on people: get a second opinion from someone you trust.

December

This month—particularly the second half—is all about home, family, and a sense of belonging, as Mars, the Sun, and Venus all move into Capricorn (on the 15th, 21st, and 24th, respectively). While all these planets move through your solar fourth house, it's time to get serious about your domestic life. What makes you feel rooted, secure, loved? What makes you feel like you belong? This is a good time for having deep conversations with family members, dealing with projects around the house that you've been putting off, or simply enjoying the comforts of home.

Moon Cycles

On the 4th, a Full Moon in Gemini may bring a long-simmering question to a head for you. If you've been longing for something *more* in life—excitement, fulfillment, or romance—your actions now could finally give you the life you've been dreaming of.

Then on the 19th, a New Moon in Sagittarius invites you to start making plans for a big adventure in your future. From researching educational programs to beginning to plan a travel itinerary, the little steps you take now will add up in a big way.

Power Days

The 7th is a lucky day for you at work: the more effort you've been putting in, the more amazing results you're likely to see. Share your feelings on the 13th! You just might find that they're reciprocated. Your self-confidence gets a boost on the 25th: to make the most of it, share your good vibes with others.

Days to Watch For

Don't settle for less than you deserve on the 14th (no matter how tempting it may seem in the moment). Watch out for jealousy (your own or someone else's) on the 21st: there's enough happiness for everyone. It might take a bit of extra effort to keep the peace (especially with family) on the 27th, but the effort will be worth it.

♏

Scorpio

The Scorpion
October 23 to November 22

Element: Water
Ruling planets: Mars (traditional) and Pluto (modern)
Keyword: Intensity
Key phrase: I question

Gemstone: Topaz
Power stones: Obsidian, garnet
Color: Black
Flower: Chrysanthemum

All about Scorpio

Strengths and Gifts

At the end of October, the Sun enters the thrilling sign of Scorpio. Following on the heels of even-tempered (but sometimes indecisive) Libra, Scorpio is passionate, focused, and determined. As a water sign named after the powerful scorpion, you feel things deeply, and you're motivated by a desire for power, truth, and emotional intensity.

♏

At first glance, Scorpio, you may come across as quiet, self-contained, and maybe even a bit brooding. Scorpio isn't the loudest or most gregarious sign in the zodiac, but the phrase "still waters run deep" may as well have been invented to describe a Scorpio. You've got a powerful, magnetic personality and a virtually bottomless well of inner strength.

That strength often shows up as sheer determination and focus. When you truly want something, Scorpio, you're single-minded about getting it. You're resourceful and strategic; if at first you don't succeed, you'll keep going until you do.

You're also not afraid of conflict. Though you're probably not the type to seek out drama for its own sake, you won't back down if you're threatened. Good luck to anybody who tries to intimidate or boss around a Scorpio: you won't take it lying down, and you won't forget it! For better or worse, nobody knows how to hold a grudge quite like a Scorpio.

Because Scorpio is so intense, people often (understandably!) mistake it for a fire sign—but, in fact, it's a water sign. Thanks to the water element, Scorpio, you're *incredibly* perceptive when it comes to other people. You're good at understanding what makes people tick, sometimes understanding others better than they do themselves.

But while you're eerily good at gazing into other people's souls, you're very private when it comes to your own business!

You're the opposite of an oversharer. With the exception of your trusted inner circle, you feel most comfortable keeping your feelings to yourself. (This is partly why Scorpios tend to carry an air of mystery!)

You're not afraid of the dark side of life (and people). You understand on an intuitive level that the universe isn't all sunshine—there are shadows, too. And while some people would prefer to bury their heads in the sand and pretend that the dark stuff doesn't exist, you value the truth, even when it isn't pretty.

Friendship and Love

You're the most intense sign of the zodiac, Scorpio, and you want your relationships to match! When you love someone, whether romantically or platonically, the most important thing to you is depth. You're not one for small talk, playing the field, or casual flings—when you're in, you're *all in*. You want passion, deep feelings, and total honesty.

Your mysterious aura is magnetically attractive, but it can also make you something of a tough nut to crack! No matter how friendly and sociable you are, people still get the impression—probably correctly!—that there's a *lot* going on beneath the surface. You won't let your guard down for just anyone; it often takes time and commitment, or a truly special connection, for you to be willing to let others see the real you.

It may take a bit of work to really get to know you, Scorpio, but it's absolutely worth it. Your love runs *deep*, and you give your close relationships your full attention. While some signs can be wishy-washy, even a bit fickle, once you decide you care about someone, you go all in. When you really fall in love, it's thrilling, passionate, and completely steamy.

You're also deeply loyal—you only give your heart to someone when you genuinely mean it. You aren't one to have your head turned every time someone interesting walks onto the scene, and you're not afraid to commit. You expect the same loyalty and commitment in return, and won't tolerate someone who keeps one foot in and one foot out of the relationship.

This means that, in your darker moments, you're highly susceptible to suspicion and jealousy, especially if you've been hurt in the past. You can even, without meaning to, end up being a bit controlling of your close friends and partners, which is something to watch out for. If you know—or even just suspect—that someone in your life has betrayed you, you're able to hold a grudge virtually forever. In close relationships, your challenge is to learn how to open up and truly trust other people.

Work and Money

As a smart, curious, and somewhat intense person, Scorpio, it's important that your work is stimulating enough to hold your attention. You probably won't be happy unless you're challenged in some way! With your interest in digging deep and finding the truth, any work with an investigative component should appeal to you—from scholar to attorney to psychologist. With your gift for strategic thinking and your interest in the workings of power, you could easily rise to the top (or pull the strings from back-stage) in government. But no matter where you work, if there are office politics at play, you're probably a whiz at navigating them.

You're most likely *very* strategic when it comes to money. You're not someone to blow your hard-earned cash on an impulse or to cross your fingers and just hope your finances all add up. You value the sense of control you get from having a plan, and from knowing exactly where every dollar is going and why. Just remember to leave room for generosity in your financial plans: helping others out is always worth it (and feels surprisingly good!).

Struggles and Growth

As much as possible, you like to stay in control. You plan care-fully, investigate everything, and keep your guard up until you're *sure* it's safe to let it down. The trouble with this is that the world is wild and unpredictable. It's impossible to plan for everything or to stay in control *all* the time. What's more, sometimes it's rewarding to act a little recklessly, to open up to new people, or just to go with the flow. Try to ease up every once in a while, and remember that you can loosen the reins and still be happy.

You also sometimes struggle with black-and-white thinking, especially in relationships. It makes things simpler to imagine that people are either all good or all bad, that they're either with you or against you—but reality is almost always more complicated. If you can give people (including yourself!) space to be their full, complex, sometimes contradictory selves—and maybe even give them a second chance every once in a while—your relationships will grow stronger and deeper.

Journaling Page

Think about your goals for 2025. Which of your Scorpio gifts—focus, passion, strategy, determination—will you call on to help you achieve them? Which elements of the Scorpio personality do you want to lean into this year?

The Year Ahead for Scorpio

The Eclipses

Every year has some eclipses—usually around four—and they tend to be some of the most significant (and often most intense) times of the year. By paying attention to them, you can get a sense of the overarching story of your year: the beginnings, endings, and surprise twists. Some will feel more personally meaningful than others—that depends on what's in your personal birth chart—but all are important. The year 2025 has four eclipses: lunar eclipses in Virgo and Pisces and solar eclipses in Aries and Virgo.

First is the Virgo lunar eclipse on March 14th. You may be faced with a crisis in your friend group or a major drama in a community organization you're part of. Your social life overall probably feels a bit chaotic right now: you may want to reevaluate your role in the group, to step in and help, or even to step back for a while.

Next up is the Aries solar eclipse on March 29th. This one invites you to begin new routines (even if you didn't think there was anything wrong with your old routines!). The important thing is to believe that it's possible to change your life for the better—and to start taking small steps.

In the fall, a Pisces lunar eclipse arrives on September 7th. This is a huge opportunity for you to let some of your barriers fall. By expressing yourself, sharing your ideas, or letting your feelings show, you can finally find the happiness you've been seeking.

Finally, the solar eclipse in Virgo on September 21st is the last eclipse of the year. There's a good chance that new people you meet right now will change your life in a lasting way. Try not to resist the change: trust that the change is happening for a reason, even if you can't yet tell what it is.

The Big Picture

The eclipses aren't the only valuable information the skies have to offer you about your year ahead. Next, look to the outer planets: Jupiter, Saturn, Uranus, Neptune, and Pluto. These five planets move slowly through the zodiac, staying in the same sign for months or even years at a time. This means that by tuning in to their movements, you can track the big-picture story of your life.

First is **Jupiter**, planet of expansion and good fortune. It begins the year in Gemini and your solar eighth house of power and transformation. With Jupiter's lucky energy in this house, you can expect positive life changes to come. This transit sometimes means that an inheritance or other financial windfall will come your way—but more generally, it means you can count on other people to support you (so don't be scared to ask!). Then on June 9th, Jupiter moves into Cancer, where it'll stay for the rest of the year. This second half of the year is an amazing time for travel—a trip to the ocean will be particularly rewarding!

Next comes **Saturn**, planet of discipline and limits. It begins the year in Pisces, moves into Aries on May 24th, and returns to Pisces on September 1st. While it's in Pisces, romantic relationships—even strong and fulfilling ones!—may feel a bit challenging. Even in the tough moments, trust that you're learning about yourself and becoming stronger. Then, when Saturn is in Aries, it's an ideal time to start working toward a new goal: think long term, not short term. Tap into your willpower, dig into the unglamorous but necessary tasks, and watch as your dreams gradually begin coming to life.

Neptune, planet of dreams and illusions, also splits its time between Pisces and Aries this year, starting off in Pisces, moving into Aries on March 30th, and returning to Pisces on October 22nd. While it's in Pisces, you may find yourself putting people—especially crushes or new partners—on a pedestal. Unrealistic expectations might cause problems in the long run, so be careful not to demand perfection of anyone. Then, when Neptune is in Aries, watch out for fad diets or weird new supplements: anything that seems too good to be true right now, especially in the realm of health and wellness, almost definitely is.

Uranus, planet of revolution and change, starts out in Taurus, moves into Gemini from July 7th through November 7th, then returns to Taurus (before moving into Gemini for the long haul in early 2026). In the time since Uranus first entered Taurus in 2018, you've probably experienced a fair amount of instability in your close relationships. Bad relationships (romantic or platonic) may have ended, but good relationships have grown stronger thanks to the challenges. Then, when Uranus enters Gemini, expect your money situation to change—especially if you share finances with someone else. Try to have some money of your own stashed away, if only for your own peace of mind.

Finally, transformational **Pluto** continues its yearslong journey through Aquarius, where it'll be until 2043. For you, this is a time to delve into your childhood, your background, or your family relationships. This may not be easy, but it's more than worthwhile. Prioritize your healing now, and you'll grow more than you even believe possible.

Your Ruling Planet

You, Scorpio, have not one but *two* ruling planets: according to traditional astrology, you're ruled by assertive Mars; according to modern astrology, you're ruled by mysterious Pluto. Choose one—or pay attention to both! In 2025, you'll want to pay particular attention to Mars retrograde, which extends from the start of the year to February 23rd. Watch out for your ego during this retrograde, especially at work! It might be tempting to confront a bad boss or start an ambitious new project, but you'll have more success if you plan now but wait until later to act. Your other ruling planet, Pluto, spends all year in Aquarius and your solar fourth house, which means themes of home, family, and your inner child will pop up a *lot* this year. Late January (when the Sun, Mercury, and the New Moon all join Aquarius in Pluto) is likely to amplify these themes even further. And October 24th, when the Sun in Scorpio squares off with Pluto, is likely to be a significant and transformative day for you.

♏

January

The new year kicks off with three retrograde planets: Mars, Jupiter, and Uranus. Jupiter and Uranus are unlikely to be too disruptive to your daily life, but while Mars is retrograde, it's smart to avoid risks or conflict—especially at work. It's also not the time for spur-of-the-moment travel, unless absolutely necessary. The Sun moves into Aquarius on the 19th, followed by Mercury on the 27th. This is a good time for conversations with family or roommates, whether you've got deep feelings to express or you just want to change up the decor.

Moon Cycles

The Cancer Full Moon on January 13th activates your adventurous side. You tend to be a bit cautious, to look before you leap—but right now, you might find it necessary, and even surprisingly healing, to let go and follow your heart.

Then the Aquarius New Moon on the 29th may leave you feeling tender and unusually vulnerable. Let this Moon remind you that you don't have to be tough *all* the time: lean on the people who love you. There's strength in softness, too.

Power Days

The 9th is likely to bring surprises (positive ones!) in your relationships, and there's a good chance you'll meet an exciting new person. The 23rd is an ideal day to assert yourself: initiate a tough conversation or ask someone out. You'll probably be extra sensitive on the 28th. Trust your feelings: they have a lot to teach you today.

Days to Watch For

Conflict with a colleague or supervisor is possible on the 2nd, but try not to get drawn into unnecessary drama. Focus on your own work. On the 7th, watch out for jealousy: paranoia could easily ruin an otherwise strong relationship! It's easy to (unintentionally) act bossy or controlling on the 21st, so make an extra effort to be generous.

February

Venus moves into Aries on the 4th: if you're in a relationship, don't worry so much about romance or thrills, just focus on doing the small stuff and being there for each other. Mercury moves into Pisces on the 14th, followed by the Sun on the 18th. Let your imagination loose! This is an ideal time for writing, creating, even signing up for an art class. Mars retrograde ends on the 23rd, which is great news! Your confidence comes roaring back now, and you're ready to take on your big goals again.

Moon Cycles

On the 12th, the Full Moon in Leo will likely make you feel like you're in the spotlight (like it or not!). Don't be scared to take on a leading role right now, and don't hide your gifts or talents away. This is your time to shine!

Then on the 27th, the Pisces New Moon could signal that a new love is on the horizon—or it could mean that it's time to give *yourself* some renewed care and attention. You've been working hard lately: make room for beauty and romance in your life, too.

Power Days

The 3rd is an ideal day for making big plans, especially when it comes to travel or a family reunion. Your judgment will be *excellent* on the 5th: this is a great day for serious conversations and committing to challenging (but exciting!) projects. On the 19th, ask for what you want directly and you're likely to get it!

Days to Watch For

Secrets—your own or someone else's—might come to light on the 4th: try to stay open-minded and don't rush to judgment. Be prepared for unexpected (maybe even unwanted) changes on the 11th: being flexible is your best bet right now. On the 12th, your judgment probably isn't the best, so don't make any hasty decisions today!

March

This month is defined by two retrogrades: Venus retrograde begins on the 1st, and Mercury retrograde starts on the 15th. Both retrogrades are likely to throw your habits and routines off somewhat. It's nothing to worry about, just a signal for you to *slow down* and take some extra care with your daily activities. Proofread your messages, double-check your schedule before you commit to anything, and get a second opinion on any bigger decisions—especially when it comes to new relationships—and you'll be fine.

Moon Cycles

Eclipse season is here! On the 14th, the lunar eclipse in Virgo is a time to help out other people in your life, from friends to classmates to neighbors. If you're given an opportunity to be of service to someone else, take it: it'll end up being rewarding for you, too.

Then on the 29th, the solar eclipse in Aries is an opportunity for you to start creating bold new plans for your life. If you've ever wished things were different—or even that *you* were different—this is a golden opportunity to take the first step toward change.

Power Days

Your confidence gets a boost on the 4th: let your enthusiasm shine and don't hold back, and people will be drawn to you! You're even more perceptive than usual on the 10th: trusting your instincts at work will lead to huge success. On the 19th, hard work will be rewarded.

Days to Watch For

Your instincts may be a little scrambled on the 3rd, especially when it comes to relationship matters. Don't hesitate to ask someone you trust for advice. Avoid making big decisions on the 9th: wait a few days if you can. Emotions are intense on the 24th, so be extra gentle with yourself.

April

Mercury retrograde ends on the 7th, and Venus retrograde ends on the 12th! After this, *no* planets are retrograde through the end of the month—a rare chance for you to go full speed ahead! Mars returns to Leo on the 18th, activating your ambition and desire for success and recognition. Chase your dreams, but watch out for power struggles and ego conflicts. The Sun enters Taurus on the 19th, kicking off a time to focus on the people closest to you. Invest energy in those you love and it'll pay off in a big way.

Moon Cycles

On the 12th, the Libra Full Moon invites you to clear negative energy from your life. If you've struggled with a habit that no longer feels good or a relationship that only seems to throw your life out of balance, this is a good chance to walk away.

The Taurus New Moon on the 27th is one of the best days of the year for beginning a meaningful new relationship. If you meet someone today—whether a friend, a crush, or something in between—don't be surprised if they end up being an important person in your life.

Power Days

Don't try to go it alone on the 1st: cooperation will bring the best results today. Your charm is amplified on the 7th: this is an ideal day for scheduling interviews, presentations, or important meetings. The 15th is a great day for romance and dating (or scheduling a date night with your partner!).

Days to Watch For

Family conflict is likely on the 13th—it isn't fun, but it's a huge opportunity to transform your relationships for the better. On the 20th, your needs might clash with your partner's: open, non-judgmental communication will help. Try to avoid arguments and power struggles on the 27th: better to walk away than to let your temper make things worse!

May

Pluto retrograde begins on the 4th. You probably won't feel this retrograde too acutely, but it's a good time to process any transformations, revelations, or intense experiences you've had over the past six months. Mercury moves into Taurus on the 10th. Between the 10th and 20th, you'll have a great opportunity to talk over any relationship problems you've been having: don't be shy about bringing these things up! Honesty and openness will deepen your connection, bring much-needed clarity—and might even be surprisingly enjoyable.

Moon Cycles

The Scorpio Full Moon on the 12th is an important time to focus on your own needs, desires, and emotions. Forget about what other people want from you for a minute—are *you* happy with the way things are going? If not, what's missing—and how can you get it?

Then the Gemini New Moon on the 26th might lead to surprisingly meaningful encounters with acquaintances—or even strangers. Expect deep conversations with people you're not typically close with. Other people have a lot to teach you about yourself today, so pay attention.

Power Days

Your idealistic side comes out on the 3rd. Forget about pessimism—let yourself dream big, and amazing things can happen! The 7th is a great day for spending time with friends: your community might surprise you in wonderful ways today. If you stay flexible and open to surprises on the 17th, your life will change for the better.

Days to Watch For

Communication with your partner or best friend is likely to get scrambled on the 10th: give each other the benefit of the doubt. Watch out for your temper on the 11th: if you're not careful, it could turn minor problems into big ones. Try to avoid big risks on the 20th—at least wait a day or two.

June

Venus moves into Taurus on the 6th, and any hard work you've put into your relationships will pay off now. It's an excellent time for finding balance, enjoying the company of the people you love, and even settling arguments or reconnecting with people you've had conflict with in the past. Mercury moves into Cancer on the 8th, followed by Jupiter on the 9th: this is an ideal time to spread your wings and expand your horizons, whether through travel, education, or simply meeting new people.

Moon Cycles

The Full Moon in Sagittarius on the 11th is likely to bring a money issue to the forefront for you. If you've been working toward a big raise or thinking about making a big purchase, this could be the time it finally happens.

Then the New Moon in Cancer on the 25th might make you feel a bit restless about your life (and relationships). If you've grown bored or complacent, now's the time to start dreaming of new adventures and to think about how you want to grow.

Power Days

You'll be extra courageous on the 1st: this is a good time to stand up for yourself, your friends, and your community. The 21st is a truly amazing day for relationships, whether you're focused on starting a new one, rekindling an old one, or strengthening an existing one. Be assertive at work on the 27th!

Days to Watch For

Any existing relationship tensions will be amplified on the 7th (but if you take this opportunity to work through things, you'll be glad you did!). You'll probably be irritable on the 8th: try not to take out your bad mood on people who don't deserve it. Impulsive actions could lead to unintended consequences on the 15th, so move with care.

July

Three retrogrades begin this month: Neptune on the 4th, Saturn on the 13th, and Mercury on the 18th. Saturn retrograde is a good time for internalizing the lessons of past challenges and struggles: be reflective and honest with yourself right now. During this Mercury retrograde, miscommunications with colleagues, clients, or even your boss are more likely than usual. If you're confused or unsure about what somebody means, don't make assumptions or jump to conclusions: *ask them*. The extra clarity will help everyone.

Moon Cycles

The Full Moon in Capricorn on the 10th is likely to feel like one of the busiest days of the year for you. You're slammed at work and your social calendar is bustling! You might be overwhelmed, but trust that it won't stay this way forever.

On the 24th, the New Moon in Leo is an opportunity for you to rethink your goals in life. Are you aiming big enough? Don't be scared to be ambitious: you're smart and talented, and there's no reason *not* to dream big!

Power Days

Take the initiative on the 5th: don't hang back or wait around for others! On the 11th, you may feel a strong need to step outside your comfort zone and do something different—listen to it. The

24th is likely to be a big career day for you: all your hard work is finally paying off.

Days to Watch For

You may experience some unexpected drama in your love life on the 4th: try to trust that change is a good thing, even if it's stressful in the moment. Your ego may take a blow on the 25th: be kind to yourself. If your self-doubt comes to the surface on the 31st, try to seek out supportive people.

August

Breathe a sigh of relief: Mercury retrograde ends on the 11th! The Sun moves into Virgo on the 22nd, shining a spotlight on your social life. Spending time in groups right now—whether that's your circle of friends, a club, or a community you're part of—should feel extra rewarding. By leaning on others for support right now, you'll accomplish *much* more than you could on your own. Finally, Venus moves into Leo on the 25th, making this an excellent time for cooperation and collaboration at work.

Moon Cycles

Under the Aquarius Full Moon on the 9th, you might find that your unique perspective puts you at odds with your family or the people you live with. Put some extra effort into understanding each other, but don't give up on your own needs for the sake of the group.

Then under the Virgo New Moon on the 23rd, make a point of getting out and socializing! You have a chance now to meet new people and make new connections. The more you feel like a part of the community today, the happier you'll be.

Power Days

The 7th is a good day for making needed changes to your home life, your routines, even the decor. You're stronger than ever on the 20th: take on the challenging tasks, projects, or conversations you've been putting off. The 26th is an ideal day for meeting new people, traveling to new places, or even starting a new job.

Days to Watch For

Arguments are likely on the 1st. Don't be afraid to say how you really feel; just try to do so with kindness. On the 14th, negative emotions can feel overwhelming. Don't suppress them, but try to talk things out with someone you trust. On the 28th, remember that you can't control other people—all you can do is support them.

September

On the 1st, Saturn moves backward into Pisces, and you may feel like you're suddenly repeating old experiences and rehashing old challenges (especially with romantic partners). Look at this as a second chance to get things right. On the 6th, Uranus retrograde begins. If you've felt like life has been changing too fast lately, things might slow down now to give you a breather. On the 22nd, Mars moves into Scorpio. Be assertive and stand up for yourself! This is your time to shine.

Moon Cycles

It's eclipse season again! On the 7th, the lunar eclipse in Pisces may shake things up in your love life. Someone new and exciting could enter your life, or you could have major revelations about how you feel. Either way, trust that things won't be boring.

Then on the 21st, the solar eclipse in Virgo may mark a major shift in the way you fit into your community. If you've felt like an outsider, you may come into your own now. If you've been experiencing conflict, you may finally find a way forward.

Power Days

The 11th is an ideal day for introducing a new partner or crush to your friend group! On the 19th, ask for help on a work project—it'll go *much* more smoothly than if you tried to do everything on your own. You're likely to have a great time socializing or traveling on the 26th.

Days to Watch For

The 12th isn't a great day for dealing with difficult situations—you might not even be seeing reality clearly right now. It's tempting to act recklessly on the 24th, but you're likely to regret it later on. Try to stay on an even keel! You may feel pessimistic on the 28th, but things should start looking up soon.

October

On the 6th, Mercury joins Mars in Scorpio, and the Sun follows on the 22nd. You'll probably feel like you're firing on all cylinders this month, especially between the 22nd and 29th. You're confident, courageous, and free to be wholly yourself. But while it's good to put yourself first every once in a while, be careful not to completely ignore the needs of the people you love! When Mercury moves into Sagittarius on the 29th, your attention may turn to financial matters. This is a great time for budgeting, planning, and negotiating.

Moon Cycles

Under the Aries Full Moon on the 6th, it's easy to make big, reckless decisions. Sometimes that's exactly what you need! Just be careful not to overcommit right now—or to impulsively choose a course of action you'll regret later on.

Under the Libra New Moon on the 21st, you can expect to feel somewhat drained. This is a time for peace and quiet, not action! Your energy is likely to be at a low point right now, so schedule some time to rest, reflect, and recharge if possible.

Power Days

The 9th is a day to have adventures with your friends: you'll learn a lot (and have fun!) if you step outside your comfort zone. You're confident and powerful on the 23rd: use this energy to make changes or stand up for yourself. Taking (calculated) risks on the 27th is likely to turn out in your favor.

Days to Watch For

Your head and your heart may be at odds on the 8th, so try to find a balance. You're likely to feel unappreciated or misunderstood at work on the 15th, but lashing out or acting passive-aggressive won't help matters. Expect some frustration with parents or an authority figure on the 24th, and don't be scared to stand up for yourself.

November

Venus moves into Scorpio on the 6th, highlighting everything that makes you most attractive. Right now, the best way to get along with others or charm your crush is simply by being yourself. The final Mercury retrograde of the year happens this month, starting on the 9th and ending on the 29th. You may make money mistakes, especially from the 9th to the 18th: set reminders so you don't forget to pay any important bills, and be careful you're sending your mobile payment to the right person!

Moon Cycles

If you've been dissatisfied with something in your relationship or quietly holding onto a secret crush, it's all likely to come out in the open under the Taurus Full Moon on the 5th. You can find real happiness if you're honest about what you want.

Then on the 20th, the Scorpio New Moon is one of the most powerful Moons of the year for you. This is your chance to start fresh, to reinvent yourself, to change your destiny. Live as though anything is possible—because right now it is!

Power Days

By being compassionate and helping others on the 3rd, you'll end up making things better for yourself, too. The 17th may be one of the luckiest days of the year for you, so get out there, make the most of it, and enjoy the good energy! Fresh confidence and self-knowledge bring popularity and success on the 19th.

Days to Watch For

Your emotions could be all over the place on the 4th, so don't make any big commitments right now: you're probably not even sure what you want. The demands of work and your personal life are in tension on the 12th, and you may need some extra self-care. Don't take loved ones for granted on the 21st—they may surprise you!

December

During the first half of the month, with the Sun and Venus in Sagittarius (and Mercury joining them on the 11th), it's a good time to get clear about your material values, whether that means redoing your budget, getting rid of clutter in your home, or buying something you really love. The second half of the month is all about spending time with other people, as Mars, the Sun, and Venus all move into Capricorn (on the 15th, 21st, and 24th, respectively). You might feel especially busy right now—try to embrace it!

Moon Cycles

The Gemini Full Moon on the 4th is likely to be a particularly intense one for you—but not in a bad way! Truths will be revealed and your life will be changed. While real transformation is rarely *easy*, it'll be worth it in the end.

On the 19th, the New Moon in Sagittarius is an ideal time to take stock of your financial situation and create a new budget or new money goals for the year ahead. Let yourself be a little optimistic and trust that abundance is possible.

Power Days

Get serious about your goals on the 7th: right now, nobody can hold you back but yourself. Carve out some alone time to reflect on the 16th, and you'll come to important realizations about who you are and what you want. The 29th is an incredible day for romance: your crush will probably find you completely charming today!

Days to Watch For

On the 2nd, it may be hard to know what (or who) you really want: be careful about making promises or commitments you won't be able to stick to. Insecurities are likely to pop up on the 20th, so lean on your friends if you need some support. Be careful not to make assumptions on the 24th—you probably don't have the full picture.

♏

♐ Sagittarius

The Archer
November 22 to December 21

Element: Fire
Ruling planet: Jupiter
Keyword: Purpose
Key phrase: I adventure

Gemstone: Turquoise
Power stones: Lapis lazuli, sodalite
Color: Purple
Flower: Narcissus

All about Sagittarius

Strengths and Gifts

The Sun enters Sagittarius, the final fire sign of the year, in late November. In contrast to private and careful Scorpio, the sign immediately preceding it in the zodiac, Sagittarius is adventurous and sometimes a bit reckless. You, Sagittarius, are driven by a desire for honesty, purpose, and higher knowledge.

You're ruled by Jupiter, planet of growth and abundance—and because of this, you possess an innate optimism. You approach the world with confidence and an open mind; you're not afraid to take risks and try new things. Even if things don't work out, you trust that you'll gain valuable experience, learn about the world, or at least come away with a good story!

With your open, optimistic nature, you prefer to be direct and straightforward. You're honest (sometimes to a fault!), and you don't see any point in beating around the bush. You won't hesitate to share your opinions—even the unpopular ones—but you aren't rigid in your thinking. When others disagree with you, you'll always listen, and you're more willing than most people to change your mind.

While some people are afraid of change, you tend to welcome it with open arms. With your adventurous spirit, you're always eager to have new experiences, meet different people, and see as much as you can of the world. (Sagittarius is the sign associated most strongly with travel.) You probably prefer adventure to routine, and you tend to get a bit restless if things stay the same for too long. If you feel like your relationship, career, or location has gotten stale or no longer has anything to teach you, you're willing to change things up at the drop of a hat.

Your freedom and independence are incredibly precious to you. It's also important for you to feel like you're constantly learning. If you feel like you no longer have the space or support to grow where you are, or if you feel like a job or person has started to impinge on your freedom, you won't hesitate to move on.

All of this can sometimes make you come across as a bit wild, Sagittarius—but you have a deeply thoughtful, philosophical bent, too. You value learning, education, and higher knowledge. You love to learn, ask questions, and talk about big ideas. There's nothing quite so thrilling as a new intellectual challenge!

Friendship and Love

With Jupiter as your ruling planet, Sagittarius, generosity is one of the guiding forces of your life—and this is particularly apparent in your relationships. You're generous not just with your resources (it brings you serious joy to cover the tab when you go out with friends), but also with your time, attention, and enthusiasm. With your warm and giving nature, you're an amazing friend and partner.

You bring an undeniable excitement to your relationships. You're up for anything: Spontaneous road trip? Spur-of-the-moment dance party? Randomly get tickets to the opera? Sounds great to you! You can make just about anything feel fun and fresh, and your easygoing spirit and sense of adventure draw people to you.

You're able to get along with most people, but the ones you'll *truly* click with are the ones who can match your energy. Someone who's overly fussy or picky, who's unwilling to change up their routines, or who simply doesn't like spontaneity is unlikely to be a good match for you in the long term. You need a partner who is just as independent as you are, and who supports and values your adventurous side.

The flip side of all this enthusiasm and fun, though, is that you're not the most organized, and can sometimes neglect the small stuff. You could be absolutely head over heels for somebody and still forget their birthday! Making a bit of extra effort when it comes to the small moments and details can make a big difference in your relationships.

You approach friendships and romantic relationships with your characteristic optimism, assuming that most people you meet are interesting and worth getting to know. You probably aren't the jealous type: because *your* intentions are good, you assume that others have good intentions, too. Sometimes you end up getting hurt because of this—not *everyone* deserves your trust.

Your optimism can also lead you to jump into relationships too quickly, when if you had waited and gotten to know the other person a bit better first you would've realized you're not actually right for each other. Practice taking your time!

Work and Money

With your intellect and curiosity, you're likely to shine as a scholar, writer, or public intellectual—really in any field that involves knowledge and ideas. You're uniquely gifted when it comes to understanding the big picture, and you would be great at helping an organization chart its overall strategy. The flip side is that you probably are not the most detail-oriented person in the world, and may struggle in roles that require you to keep lots of small stuff organized. Sagittarius is also the sign most strongly associated with travel, and you'd find fulfillment in a job that lets you travel the country—even the world.

Everybody worries about money a little (or a lot), but thanks to your optimistic side, there's probably a part of you that has faith that things will "just work out." You may struggle to keep a detailed budget, preferring just to look at the big picture instead. But you'd likely benefit from paying a bit more attention to the nitty-gritty—from the line items in your budget to the details of your 401k. It may put you in a better position overall!

Struggles and Growth

To your credit, you're not an overly controlling person: you understand that there's much in the universe that's simply out of your hands. Sometimes, though, this means that you leave things too much up to chance. As good as you are at winging it, there are situations that call for effort, preparation, and careful planning! From your relationships to your finances to your career, make a point every once in a while to actually take ownership of your life and decisions, and to plan—to the extent that it's possible—for the future.

Your honesty is one of the very best things about you: other people never need to guess what you're thinking or where they stand with you. Being open about what you're feeling—good *or* bad—makes it possible to address issues as they arise and to keep lines of communication clear. Sometimes, though, you're a little *too* blunt, accidentally hurting others with your words. If you can remember to think before you speak, you may find that your relationships get stronger.

Journaling Page

Think about your goals for 2025. Which of your Sagittarius gifts—intellect, adventurousness, honesty, optimism—will you call on to help you achieve them? Which elements of the Sagittarius personality do you want to lean into this year?

The Year Ahead for Sagittarius

The Eclipses

When you're planning for the year ahead, one of the most important things you can do is look to the eclipses, which mark major moments of transition and change. While eclipses happen every year—2025, like most years, has four of them, two in Virgo and one each in Aries and Pisces—they'll all affect you differently. Some might feel practically earth-shattering, and some will be hardly noticeable! It all depends on your personal birth chart.

The 2025 eclipses begin with a lunar eclipse in Virgo on March 14th. For you, this one's likely to signal important changes in your professional life. You might experience shake-ups or emergencies at work, or you could finally be pushed to make the career change you've been dreaming of.

Two weeks later comes a solar eclipse in fiery Aries on the 29th. This one's likely to be particularly creatively fertile for you: expect to be struck by new inspiration or to begin work on a new project. Don't pressure yourself to get results right now; just focus on following your imagination where it leads.

September brings the third and fourth eclipses of 2025. The lunar eclipse in Pisces arrives on the 7th and is likely to highlight any issues that have been happening at home. From home maintenance issues to family drama, now is the time to see the issue clearly, discuss it honestly, and put any lingering problems to bed.

Finally, the Virgo solar eclipse falls on September 21st. Back in March, the Virgo lunar eclipse probably marked changes, transitions, or even endings related to your job or career. Now this eclipse offers you a new path to move forward. Don't worry if you don't have all the answers yet. You don't need total clarity; you just need to keep going, putting one foot in front of the other.

The Big Picture

In addition to the eclipses, you can find important info about your year ahead in the movement of the outer planets: Jupiter, Saturn, Uranus, Neptune, and Pluto. These five planets move slowly through the zodiac, spending months (and often years!) at a time in the same sign. In contrast to the inner planets, which are better at illuminating your day-to-day moods and activities, the outer planets have a lot to teach about the big picture.

First up is **Jupiter**, planet of growth and abundance—and, Sagittarius, your ruling planet! Jupiter is a good indicator of where you'll experience luck (or how you can create your own luck) in the year ahead. It spends roughly the first half of 2025 in Gemini and your solar seventh house of partnership. Work collaboratively with others, and amazing things will happen (you might just be lucky in love, too!). Then on June 9th, Jupiter moves into Cancer, where it'll stay for the rest of the year.

During this period, sharing your resources with friends or your community is likely to bring good luck back to you.

The next of the outer planets is **Saturn**. The planet of responsibility and restrictions splits its time this year between Pisces and Aries: it starts out in Pisces, moves into Aries on May 24th, and returns to Pisces on September 1st. While it's in Pisces, it's important for you to deal with issues in your home and inner life. Whether you're working through problems in therapy or putting effort into mending relationships with family members, it won't be easy, but it *will* be worth it. While Saturn is in Aries, you may feel a bit less gregarious or creative than usual. Especially if your career is in a creative field, you'll have to rely on hard work, not just inspiration.

Neptune, planet of dreams and confusion, also splits its time between Pisces and Aries this year, starting the year in Pisces, entering Aries on March 30th, and returning to Pisces on October 22nd. While it's in Pisces, you may find yourself fantasizing about an ideal home or putting someone else's family on a pedestal. Try to remember that *nobody* has a perfect family life. When Neptune enters Aries, be careful about getting involved with people who idealize *you*! It feels good at first, but ultimately you need someone who sees you as a full, flawed human being.

Uranus, the most unpredictable of all the planets, spends much of 2025 in Taurus (though it dips into Gemini from July 7th through November 7th, then moves into Gemini for the long haul in early 2026). It's been in Taurus since 2018, so this is a continuation of a story that's been going on for a while now. For you, Uranus in Taurus has been a great time to alter your habits and daily routines—for instance, experimenting with a vegetarian diet or trying out new exercise routines. It's also a great time to change jobs or make changes at your existing job. If you feel dissatisfied with your work, feel empowered to make big changes now. Then, once Uranus enters Gemini, be prepared for shake-ups and conflict—but also excitement—in your closest relationships, both romantic and platonic.

Finally, **Pluto**—the most distant and slowest-moving of the planets—continues its yearslong journey through Aquarius, where it'll be until 2043. This year, let Pluto empower you to ask big questions, reflect on your own assumptions and biases, and search for deeper meaning in life. You're hungry for knowledge and truth right now, and you can find it in even the most surprising places.

Your Ruling Planet

Your ruling planet, Sagittarius, is Jupiter: planet of luck, abundance, and growth. This is part of what makes you so optimistic and generous! It also means you'll want to pay particular attention to this year's two Jupiter retrogrades, which run from the start of the year to February 4th, and November 11th through the end of the year. Unlike, say, Mercury retrograde, Jupiter retrograde is rarely very disruptive to daily life—partly because the outer planets' retrogrades all tend to be a bit milder, and partly because lucky Jupiter is benevolent even when it's moving backward! Think of this instead as a useful chance for you to step back, reflect, and look at your life with a fresh perspective. It's easy for you to get overconfident, to trust people you shouldn't, or simply to move through life so fast that you miss important information! During the year's two Jupiter retrogrades, you have the opportunity to reassess and come away with a more realistic picture.

January

The year 2025 kicks off with three retrograde planets: Mars, Jupiter, and Uranus. If possible, try to avoid travel during this Mars retrograde—especially before January 6th, when Mars moves backward from Leo into Cancer. When Venus moves into Pisces on the 2nd, it's an ideal time to take it easy and rest up at home. (It's also a good time to redecorate your living space.) Once the Sun moves into Aquarius on the 19th, followed by Mercury on the 27th, expect life to get *busy*!

Moon Cycles

The first important lunar event of 2025 is the Cancer Full Moon on January 13th. This Moon is likely to be emotionally intense, and arguments about money are possible. The key is to resist jealousy and competitiveness, and focus on working together instead.

You can expect to learn something new or find yourself drawn to new subjects under the Aquarius New Moon on the 29th. As you set intentions for the days ahead, remember that it's okay if you don't already have the answers: let your curiosity guide you.

Power Days

Giving *and* receiving support will make you feel good on the 4th—be generous with your friends, and don't be afraid to ask for help if you need it. Step outside your comfort zone on the 18th: it'll lead to good things. Even seemingly casual conversations can lead to deeper understanding and intimacy on the 24th.

Days to Watch For

Don't drop hints or beat around the bush on the 6th: if you want to be understood, you'll have to be straightforward. You're likely to feel lonely or insecure on the 10th: be careful not to act jealous or possessive, or it'll only make things worse. Watch your bank balance on the 14th, when it will be easy to overspend (especially on dates!).

February

Jupiter retrograde ends on the 4th: if you've been sitting back and reflecting, it's time to join the action again! Venus moves into Aries on the 4th, making this a great time for socializing, flirting, and dating. Mercury and the Sun both enter Pisces this month (on the 14th and 18th, respectively). You may find yourself feeling particularly nostalgic right now, but while it's healthy to reflect on the past, make sure you're not neglecting the life and relationships you have in the present.

Moon Cycles

On the 12th, the Leo Full Moon may push you to set out on a new journey or take a risk. Try to put self-doubt and uncertainty to the side, at least for now. Bet on yourself, and the universe will probably reward you.

Then on the 27th, the Pisces New Moon invites you to consider what really makes you feel secure, protected, and at home. Remind yourself that as much as you love adventure, there's nothing wrong with sometimes prioritizing the people and places that make you feel safe.

Power Days

You're extraordinarily perceptive and sensitive on the 1st: this is an excellent time to have conversations about family issues (and maybe even learn about family secrets). The 6th is an exceptional day for negotiations: everyone's likely to come out a winner. If you've had family or roommate issues, you can find a solution on the 28th.

Days to Watch For

The 8th isn't the best day for hard work or big decisions: you're feeling dreamy and sensitive, so you may not see matters clearly. You're likely to be worried about your performance at work on the 15th—but chances are, this is just your insecurities talking. On the 20th, simmering tensions (especially about housework!) may come to a head: talk things through.

March

Venus retrograde begins on the 1st, making this a less than ideal time for starting new relationships. It's also a good idea to avoid making big impulse purchases right now—you're likely to wind up wishing you hadn't spent the money! Mercury retrograde also begins on the 15th. Especially if you're dating, this Mercury retrograde is likely to lead to some miscommunications. The best way to avoid this is to *ask* what the other person wants or how they're feeling. Don't assume!

Moon Cycles

Eclipse season is here! On the 14th, the lunar eclipse in Virgo is likely to make a big splash in your professional life. If you've been hesitating to make a change, or you're unsure about next steps, this eclipse may give you the push you've needed.

Then on the 29th, the solar eclipse in Aries serves as a reminder that play and fun are just as important as work. Especially if you've been taking yourself too seriously lately, this is a sign that your creative side needs attention.

Power Days

Emotions are especially intense on the 5th. If you have deep feelings for someone, it's a good time to tell them. The 14th should bring some much-needed excitement your way—and the more you try new things and talk to new people, the more rewarding it will be. The 20th is likely to be romantic, so think about scheduling a date today!

Days to Watch For

It's easy to overcommit yourself to projects or relationships on the 2nd: be honest (including with yourself) about what you're really able to offer. Arguments are likely on the 6th: your best bet isn't trying to avoid tension, but to work through it. You're probably going to feel exhausted on the 12th, so plan on an evening in, if possible.

April

Both of the retrogrades that began in March wrap up this month: Mercury stations direct on the 7th, and Venus on the 12th. After this, *no* planets are retrograde through the end of the month— a rare opportunity to go full speed ahead! Mars moves back into Leo on the 18th, which means this is likely an excellent opportunity for travel. When Mercury and Venus both move into Aries (on the 16th and 30th, respectively), fill up your social calendar: time spent with your friends will be extra rewarding right now.

Moon Cycles

We all have to balance our personal needs with the needs of our communities—and under the Libra Full Moon on the 12th, you'll notice if your balance has been thrown out of whack. If you've been neglecting yourself (or your friends), this is your reminder to change that.

Then the Taurus New Moon on the 27th invites you to pay a bit more attention to your body and health. Have you been caring for yourself or neglecting your physical needs? If you need to treat yourself better, this is an ideal time to start.

Power Days

The sweeter and more generous you are with others on the 2nd, the more generous they'll be toward you in return. The 24th is a lovely day for socializing—especially for having friends over to your place. On the 29th, you'll be exceptionally good at understanding others, treating them with compassion, and working together to get great results.

Days to Watch For

Don't be surprised if you feel a bit grouchy on the 3rd: just take it easy and treat yourself with kindness. On the 10th, you may get frustrated with the current direction of your life or relationships—but wait a few days before taking action. If self-doubt crops up on the 18th, it'll help to surround yourself with supportive people.

May

This month puts the focus squarely on your close relationships, with the Sun entering Gemini on the 20th, followed by Mercury on the 25th. There's a good chance you'll meet someone who ends up being important to you—whether that's a future spouse, a new best friend, or even a potential business partner. Serious, one-on-one conversations will be more productive and rewarding than ever right now. Working closely with someone else, listening to their ideas, and even engaging in some good-natured debate will take you much further than you'd get on your own.

Moon Cycles

The Scorpio Full Moon on the 12th is likely to feel exhausting: you'll notice the ways you've been overloading yourself or taking on more than you can emotionally handle. This is your chance to let some things drop for the sake of your mental health.

On the 26th, a New Moon in Gemini is a beautiful opportunity to mend relationships with partners or close friends if they've grown distant or strained. With some open, honest, nonjudgmental communication, it's possible to turn over a new leaf.

Power Days

Give yourself permission to daydream on the 13th, and you may come up with genuinely useful ideas! The 22nd is a great day for connecting with people: you're excellent at reading the room and picking up on others' feelings right now. Talk through relationship problems on the 26th: you may finally find a solution that makes both of you happy.

Days to Watch For

Everything at work may feel *off* on the 5th: trust that it isn't you and things will settle down soon. You may get uncharacteristically pessimistic on the 7th, but it's important not to take any drastic action about it. If anyone (especially a partner) tries to tell you what to do on the 15th, there's likely to be conflict.

June

When Mercury and the Sun enter Cancer this month (on the 8th and 20th, respectively), it's a good time for diving deep into your feelings—maybe even beginning (or restarting) therapy. Inner work is never easy, but it's necessary, and will ultimately make you feel better. When Mars enters Virgo on the 17th, it's a great time to make big strides in your career. When you believe in yourself and ask for what you deserve, you'll be amazed by what happens. (Just be careful to avoid unnecessary conflict with colleagues!)

Moon Cycles

The Full Moon in Sagittarius on the 11th is one of the most potent lunar events of the year for you. Your emotions are overflowing, and it's important to express yourself. Outbursts are possible—but they just might lead to real relief.

On the 25th, the New Moon in Cancer is a time for you to share your deepest feelings with others. It can be tempting to avoid talking about your vulnerabilities, but right now, you have a chance to build true intimacy by opening up.

Power Days

On the 8th, it becomes easier to connect with people different from yourself: make the most of it by reaching out. The 22nd is an outstanding day for making strides in your career: you're hardworking *and* lucky today. You'll be charming, persuasive, and popular on the 29th—an ideal day for meetings, interviews, and presentations.

Days to Watch For

Working productively with colleagues and bosses might be difficult on the 2nd: if there are unspoken tensions getting in the way, best to discuss them openly. On the 4th, you may accidentally rub people the wrong way: be mindful of others' feelings! If someone hurts your feelings on the 18th, remember that you're allowed to speak up about it.

July

When Venus enters Gemini on the 4th, the focus shifts to romance. This is an ideal time to express your feelings, begin new relationships, or smooth things out if an existing relationship has gotten rocky. Most of all, it's a time to enjoy love! The second Mercury retrograde of the year kicks off on the 18th and ends on August 11th. You're especially likely to run into travel problems during this period, so avoid scheduling any big trips right now if you can—and if you can't (life happens!), book refundable tickets and have a plan B.

Moon Cycles

On the 10th, the Full Moon in Capricorn is likely to bring money issues into focus. This could mean an argument about joint finances, an unexpected bill—or a surprising windfall. If a problem has been brewing for some time, this is a good chance to put it to bed.

You'll probably feel restless under the New Moon in Leo on the 24th. You may feel that your life is boring, your routines stifling. Planning a trip, getting serious about applying to grad school, or starting another new project will help you snap out of it.

Power Days

The 1st is a great day to meet new people: you might be surprised by how well you connect with someone very different from you. On the 6th, let your imagination roam free—you'll also have a firm handle on how to feasibly turn your dreams into reality. The 20th is an ideal day to take care of business.

Days to Watch For

You may be a bit irritable on the 7th: try to avoid getting drawn into any unnecessary conflicts or taking out your feelings on the wrong people. On the 14th, you may clash with family members or roommates—turn to a partner or close friend for support. Ego could cause relationship problems on the 23rd, but try to compromise.

August

Mercury retrograde ends on the 11th, and travel should get much easier (and more enjoyable!) now. The Sun enters Virgo on the 22nd, kicking off a monthlong period for you to focus on your bigger life goals. Are you on the right path in your career? Are you happy with the way others see you? Are you making the most of your unique skills and talents? If the answer to any of these questions is no, this is an ideal time for you to be honest—with yourself and others—about what you want to change.

Moon Cycles

The Aquarius Full Moon on the 9th may end up being one of the busiest days of the year for you. If you feel overwhelmed by tasks, social engagements, or even emails, don't worry! It won't last forever—you just have to get through the next couple of days.

On the 23rd, the New Moon in Virgo is an excellent day to set career goals and intentions. Don't just go with the flow right now—get serious about deciding what kind of life you want, and make a plan to make it happen.

Power Days

You're confident and capable on the 3rd: if you apply yourself, you can make huge strides toward your goals today. On the 10th, you'll be surprised at how helpful it is to simply *listen* to people. Close relationships may go through some ups and downs on the 16th: you might argue, get closer, or a little of both.

Days to Watch For

You can stand up for yourself on the 5th (especially if you're being disrespected at work), but pick your battles wisely. On the 23rd, you may run into career barriers: don't get discouraged, but think creatively about ways around them. On the 31st, tension with authority figures might cause stress in your life!

September

On the 2nd, Mercury joins the Sun in Virgo, making this a great time to talk to others (from friends to your boss) about your career goals. You might be surprised by the light others can shed on your question. Then on the 18th, Mercury enters Libra, and on the 22nd, the Sun joins it. The most important area of your life now is your friends and community: What role are you playing in the larger group? How are you balancing your own needs with the needs of those around you?

Moon Cycles

The second eclipse season of 2025 arrives with the Pisces lunar eclipse on the 7th. There's a good chance that issues with family or roommates will arise—but you can trust that by dealing with things now, your living situation will ultimately improve.

Then the solar eclipse in Virgo on the 21st might continue to shake up your professional life. You could get a bit overwhelmed with new tasks dropping into your lap—but if you rise to the occasion, unexpected (and exciting) opportunities might come your way, too.

Power Days

The 12th is a great day to take on challenging projects: with a positive mindset, you can do virtually anything today. Inspiration strikes on the 26th: it's an ideal time to focus on a creative project. The 27th is a particularly rewarding day to participate in group activities, from community meetings to marches to parties.

Days to Watch For

Thoughts and feelings could clash on the 7th, and it may be hard to balance the demands of your career and your home life. One-on-one conversations on the 14th may leave you feeling misunderstood: don't be afraid to clarify things if you need to! Your impatience could get you in trouble on the 20th: focus on the long game.

October

Mercury and the Sun both enter Scorpio this month: Mercury on the 6th, then the Sun on the 22nd. You're likely going to need some peace and quiet right now, especially between the 22nd and 29th. Don't push yourself to get out there or be active if you're just not feeling it: you deserve a moment to reflect and recharge on your own. Once Mercury enters Sagittarius on the 29th, things may pick up a bit, and you'll feel ready to take on the world again.

Moon Cycles

On the 6th, the Full Moon in Aries should make your life feel rich, dramatic, and exciting. If you've had (or been the object of!)

a simmering, slow-burn crush this year, there's a good chance that things will reach a climax today.

There's a strong chance that new friends will enter your life under the Libra New Moon on the 21st. Your job isn't to try to *make* anything happen right now, but simply to be open to whatever new connections may find you today.

Power Days

Make a point of helping others on the 5th: it'll bring good luck your way, too. The 8th is an excellent time to negotiate a raise (or anything else) at work. It's important not to be bored on the 10th! Consider trying something new, especially with a partner or best friend.

Days to Watch For

Mistakes are likely on the 16th, especially if you're rushing! Do your best to slow down, take the time you need, and avoid jumping to conclusions. The 24th is *not* the day to make big decisions: wait a day or two if you can. Be careful not to let other people's bad moods drag you down on the 26th.

November

The last Mercury retrograde of the year begins on the 9th and ends on the 29th, and the best thing to do right now is simply slow down. If you take the time you need and refuse to be rushed, you'll be just fine. Lots of planets enter Sagittarius this month: Mars, the Sun, and Venus (on the 4th, 21st, and 30th, respectively). Even with Mercury retrograde, you're likely to feel like you're firing on all cylinders! Don't trample on anyone else's needs or opinions, but give yourself permission to express yourself freely and be true to yourself.

Moon Cycles

A health issue might come to your attention under the Taurus Full Moon on the 5th—but more likely, you'll just feel compelled to take your health more seriously. Do something to care for yourself today, whether it's eating a good meal or just getting a full night's sleep.

You're likely to feel exhausted, for no particular reason, under the Scorpio New Moon on the 20th. Avoid scheduling any strenuous activities today, if at all possible: the best thing you can do for yourself is simply rest and recharge.

Power Days

On the 2nd, you have the strength and conviction to start new projects and see them through. It's an especially good day for home improvement work. On the 12th, you're not afraid of anything! It's a good day to stand up for yourself; just don't start any unnecessary conflict. The 30th is an ideal time for dating and romance.

Days to Watch For

Your energy may be erratic on the 4th: take a moment to breathe if you find yourself getting worked up! You're likely to feel lonely and unappreciated on the 22nd, but things aren't really as bad as you're imagining right now. If you're frustrated by family or roommates on the 28th, give yourself permission to vent to your friends.

December

The first half of December remains focused on you, Sagittarius, but midway through the month, you'll feel a shift as planets begin entering Capricorn: Mars on the 15th, the Sun on the 21st, and Venus on the 24th. This is an excellent time for you to pay attention to your material values and your finances, whether that means reworking your budget, figuring out a savings plan that will actually work for you, or just investing in something you've been wanting to buy for a while.

Moon Cycles

On the 4th, the Gemini Full Moon highlights any conflicts that have put a strain on your close relationships (especially with your partner). Avoiding the issue today will only make things worse, but being honest about your needs will bring you closer together.

Finally, on the 19th, the New Moon in Sagittarius offers you a fresh start. This is one of the most powerful days of the year for setting new intentions and changing your life. If you act like anything is possible today, you just might find that it's true.

Power Days

The 9th is a great day for travel: even a short day trip is likely to be fun and give you a confidence boost. On the 18th, it's possible to heal old wounds and finally find closure with an old relationship. The 28th is an ideal day for opening up about your feelings (especially to a crush!).

Days to Watch For

The 8th is not the best day for taking risks: right now, best to keep your head down and move slowly and steadily. The 16th may be one of those days where things just don't seem to go your way. Do your best and don't blame yourself. Energy is low on the 20th: get plenty of rest if you can.

♑ Capricorn

The Goat
December 21 to January 20

Element: Earth
Ruling planet: Saturn
Keyword: Discipline
Key phrase: I achieve

Gemstone: Garnet
Power stones: Peridot, black obsidian
Color: Black
Flower: Carnation

All about Capricorn

Strengths and Gifts

The winter solstice marks the Sun's entrance into Capricorn, the last earth sign of the year. Compared to outgoing, spontaneous, restless Sagittarius, the sign immediately preceding it in the zodiac, Capricorn is much more grounded. You, Capricorn, are driven by a desire to achieve—and you have the strength, discipline, and resourcefulness to turn your dreams into reality.

Capricorn is one of the hardest-working signs of the zodiac. Thanks to your ruling planet of Saturn, you have an unmatched work ethic and focus. You're not one to wait around for a stroke of luck, a flash of inspiration, or the perfect moment to act—you understand that to get real results, you need to strategize, stay disciplined, and commit to the long haul.

You're incredibly goal-oriented. Unlike some of the other earth signs, you're unlikely to find satisfaction simply in doing your work well: you want to make things *happen*! Whether your aim is to make money, rise to the top of your field, or make the world a better place, you won't be satisfied until you get real, tangible results. While some people make decisions based on vibes or intuition, you're probably the type who wants to see the real, hard numbers.

This can make you come across as a bit pessimistic, even a naysayer, to some—especially to people who are a bit flighty or dreamy. In fact, though, you're simply a realist. Because you're so committed to your goals, you want to be honest about the difficulties that will lie along the way. Some people prefer to sugarcoat unpleasant truths, but not you. You don't sit around vaguely wishing for things to "just work out"—you understand that in order to have the beautiful life you want, it'll take some effort, and you aren't afraid to put in the legwork.

While some Capricorns may seem a bit buttoned-up at first glance, this is a sign with a secret wild side. When the workday is over and the circumstances are right, *nobody* knows how to have a good time better than you, Capricorn! Sometimes you may need a bit of extra encouragement to let loose, but remember that it's important! Especially for somebody as diligent and determined as you are, it's important to have a release every once in a while—and to remind yourself that life isn't *all* about work.

Friendship and Love

Anyone should count themselves lucky to have someone like you in their life, Capricorn. When it comes to friendship and love, you're caring, committed, and willing to put in the work to build strong, lasting, fulfilling relationships.

You value security in both romantic and platonic relationships. It's important to you to know where you stand with others and trust that you're on the same page. While some people find relationship drama to be exciting, even invigorating, you prefer steadiness. This emphatically does *not* mean that your relationships are boring, or that there's no room for change; it simply means that you value relationships where you and the other person can grow, change, and build a beautiful life *together*.

The people you're drawn to tend to be just as ambitious as you are. This doesn't mean they need to be career-obsessed—the important thing is that they have something they're passionate about, a long-term goal they're working toward, a big vision for what they want their life to look like. In the best-case scenario, you and your friends or partner can help each other along the way.

You can, however, be a bit of a tough nut to crack, particularly in the early days of friendships and romantic relationships. On the outside, you may even appear to be unconcerned with love altogether. You're not the needy type (far from it!), and you don't tend to gush or wear your emotions on your sleeve. Because you don't often let your romantic side show, some people mistakenly think you don't have one at all!

But that's not really the truth. You feel just as deeply as anyone—sometimes even *more* deeply—and you treat relationships with the seriousness they deserve. You're not the fickle type. Your love, for your friends and your partners alike, is steady, abiding, and true. The key, for you, is to make sure to open up every once in a while, even if it feels vulnerable or unnatural. Nobody can read your mind. Sometimes you have to *tell* the people you love just how much they mean to you.

Work and Money

With Saturn as your ruling planet, you're driven, disciplined, and highly motivated by a desire for external recognition. Your reputation is important to you, and you value prestige, awards, and public acclaim. There's a bit of a stereotype that all Capricorns thrive in the business world, making deals and getting rich—but that's not the full story. You can find Capricorns in every field, from business to government to the arts and beyond. Whatever kind of work you choose to do, Capricorn, the most important thing is that you're working toward a goal that matters to you.

When it comes to money, you might be the most pragmatic of all the signs. Even if you're not driven by wealth for its own sake, you understand that money will influence all other parts of your life, so you do your best to make smart decisions about earning, saving, and investing for your future. Just remember that it's not possible to plan for *everything*, and there's a lot that's outside of your control. We all make impulse purchases and experience unexpected bumps in the road sometimes. Don't blame yourself!

Struggles and Growth

You, Capricorn, are an absolute force of nature: you know how to turn big dreams into reality, how to get things done, how to change the world. In the outer world, you're unstoppable! In your *inner* world, though—the realm of your moods, feelings, and personal desires—you're not quite as comfortable. Sometimes you struggle to express your emotions to others; sometimes even *you* don't entirely know what you're feeling. But your inner life is every bit as important as the face you show to the world, so don't neglect it. Time spent working to understand yourself better is well worth it.

It's also important for you to remind yourself to take your foot off the gas every so often. When you get laser-focused on being productive or making progress toward your big goals, it's all too easy to miss out on the small, sweet moments right in front of you. You don't always need to "use" your time: sometimes it's enough just to enjoy it!

Journaling Page

Think about your goals for 2025. Which of your Capricorn gifts—discipline, integrity, pragmatism, ambition—will you call on to help you achieve them? Which elements of the Capricorn personality do you want to lean into this year?

The Year Ahead for Capricorn

The Eclipses

As you make your plans for 2025, there are a few key astrological indicators that can help you get a picture of the year to come. One of the best ways to start is to look to the eclipses. The year 2025 has four of them: two in Virgo, one in Aries, and one in Pisces. These eclipses mark major moments of transition and change in your year. They are beginnings, endings, and turning points—and depending on what's in your birth chart, their effects may be subtle or they may change practically everything!

The first eclipse of the year is the lunar eclipse in Virgo on March 14th. For you, this one's likely to mark a moment of possibility. Will you seize this opportunity to step outside of your five-year plan or your everyday routines in order to find adventure?

Two weeks later, a solar eclipse in fiery Aries on March 29th opens the door to a new phase in your home or family life. Especially if you've been dealing with drama with your loved ones or some kind of family secret, this is a chance to turn over a new leaf.

On September 7th, the lunar eclipse in Pisces is likely to make your life feel *very* hectic. Don't be surprised if lots of people suddenly dump all their feelings on you! The key is to keep your cool, don't let anyone rush you into action, and schedule some quiet time to rest.

Finally, the Virgo solar eclipse happens on September 21st. Back in March, the Virgo *lunar* eclipse probably brought drama and adventure to your life. Now that the dust has settled—at least a little bit—this is a day for you to process the lessons from it all, and move forward as a wiser, more thoughtful, more intentional version of yourself.

The Big Picture

The eclipses aren't the only important clues to what your 2025 will look like. Next, let's take a look at the movement of the outer planets of Jupiter, Saturn, Uranus, Neptune, and Pluto. These five planets move slowly through the zodiac, spending months (and often years!) at a time in the same sign. In contrast to the inner planets, which are better at illuminating your day-to-day moods and activities, the five outer planets can offer a road map for the bigger picture of your year.

First up is **Jupiter**, planet of confidence, expansiveness, and abundance. By tracking the travels of Jupiter, you can get a good sense of what kind of luck you'll have in the year ahead—and, more importantly, how to create your own luck. Jupiter spends roughly the first half of 2025 in Gemini and your solar sixth house of work and routine. Tap into Jupiter's good luck by putting your head down and doing your work—*without* any ego.

Then on June 9th, Jupiter moves into Cancer, where it'll stay for the rest of the year. If you're looking for love, chances are good that you'll finally find what you've been seeking after Jupiter enters this sign.

The next of the outer planets is **Saturn**, planet of discipline and responsibility—and your ruling planet, Capricorn! It splits its time this year between Pisces and Aries, starting out in Pisces, moving into Aries on May 24th, and returning to Pisces on September 1st. While it's in Pisces, there's a good chance you'll feel stressed by your social circle, but if you make an effort to invest in these relationships, it'll pay off in the end. Then Saturn in Aries is a good time to rearrange your living situation, mend fences with family, or delve into your own emotions. Treat your private life like it's every bit as important as your professional life—because it is.

Neptune, planet of dreams and confusion, also splits its time between Pisces and Aries this year, starting the year in Pisces, entering Aries on March 30th, and returning to Pisces on October 22nd. While it's in Pisces, there's an added possibility for misunderstandings, especially with acquaintances and neighbors, so make an extra effort to communicate clearly. Then, when Neptune enters Aries, misunderstandings are more likely to arise with family members or roommates. The more you expect others to read your mind, the more confusion is likely to arise!

Uranus, the most unpredictable of all the planets, spends much of 2025 in Taurus (though it dips into Gemini from July 7th through November 7th, then moves into Gemini for the long haul in early 2026). It's been in Taurus since 2018, so this is a continuation of a story that's been going on for a while now. For you, Uranus in Taurus has the potential to be filled with new and exciting experiences and relationships. Spending time with people who are different from you will be more rewarding than ever. If you've been looking for a new job or a change in routine, Uranus in Gemini may provide it! Just do your best to be smart, not reckless, in any changes you make.

Finally, **Pluto**—the most distant and slowest-moving of the planets—continues its yearslong journey through Aquarius, where it'll be until 2043. For you, this means that you're undergoing a major shift in your values. This is a chance for you to reconsider what you need to be happy, what you want to spend your money on, and what principles you're willing to stand up for.

Your Ruling Planet

Your ruling planet, Capricorn, is Saturn—planet of discipline, limitations, and structure. This is part of what makes you so goal-oriented, pragmatic, and focused, and the more you can tap into Saturn's energy this year, the more you'll tap into your own power. (In 2024, January 4th is a great day for leaning into your confident, authoritative side, while June 22nd is a day for overcoming major obstacles.) You'll also benefit from paying attention to Saturn's movements through the zodiac. In particular, watch for Saturn retrograde, which runs from July 13th to November 27th this year. That may sound like an intimidatingly long time—but Saturn retrograde isn't such a bad thing! For you especially, this is a powerful time to reflect on your responsibilities and ambitions. If you've taken on too much work, or if you feel you're not really doing what *you* want to do with your life, you have the chance now to course-correct.

January

The year 2025 kicks off with three retrograde planets: Mars, Jupiter, and Uranus. Of these three, Mars is the most likely to make itself known in your daily life. Watch out in particular for power struggles and ego conflict with people close to you. Maybe even more importantly, though, the year starts off with the Sun in your home sign of Capricorn! Communication planet Mercury also enters Capricorn on the 8th. This is an ideal time to focus on your needs, desires, and feelings. Forget about what other people expect of you. What do *you* want?

Moon Cycles

The first important lunar event of 2025 is the Cancer Full Moon on the 13th. For you, this Moon is likely to highlight a conflict with someone you love. Ultimately, though, this is a *good* thing: it's a chance to acknowledge the problem and work through it.

Then on the 29th, the Aquarius New Moon is an ideal time to think creatively about what will *really* make you happy. You don't have to stick to the old ways of doing things. If you've got a wild or unconventional idea, why not see it through?

Power Days

After the holidays and the start of the new year, the 4th is an ideal day to get your head on straight and start getting things done again. Stay open to new experiences (and people!) on the

13th. Don't sit around at home on the 18th if you can help it: it's is a beautiful day for adventures.

Days to Watch For

Watch out for tension with family members or roommates on the 6th. Your head and your heart might be in conflict on the 12th—don't rush to make any big decisions as you sort out your true feelings. Arguments with a partner or best friend might come up on the 15th: try to talk things through with an open mind.

February

When Venus moves into Aries on the 4th, it's an ideal time to redecorate your living space, host cozy and intimate dinner parties, or even invite your crush over for the first time. Your social life's likely to pick up when Mercury and the Sun enter Pisces (on the 14th and 18th, respectively)—be careful not to double-book yourself! Finally, unanticipated conflict with loved ones becomes a lot less likely after Mars retrograde ends on the 23rd: if close relationships have gotten strained, now's a good time to patch things up.

Moon Cycles

On the 12th, the Leo Full Moon is a day for giving *and* receiving support. You're sometimes too proud to ask for anything from your friends (you prefer to be the one *giving* help!), but it's important to let others lend a hand every once in a while, too.

Life may get extra busy for you—in a good way!—under the Pisces New Moon on the 27th. Expect chance encounters, unexpectedly meaningful conversations, and surprising coincidences. Keep your eyes open, and you'll find some extra magic in your everyday life today.

Power Days

You may experience a lucky coincidence or stroke of good fortune on the 2nd, especially one related to finances or friendship. The 9th is an ideal day to ask your crush out or finally make a commitment in your relationship. Follow your instincts on the 24th—even if they don't make rational sense.

Days to Watch For

Relationship insecurities could make you act out on the 3rd: try not to give in to your worst fears. You'll probably feel unmotivated on the 8th, so avoid scheduling important tasks or events today if you can! You may be uncharacteristically irritable on the 16th: just try not to take your bad mood out on people you love.

March

This month's going to be largely shaped by two retrogrades: Venus retrograde, which begins on the 1st, and Mercury retrograde, which starts on the 15th. For you, Capricorn, these retrogrades are particularly likely to trigger misunderstandings with family members or roommates, but you should be able to avoid major problems by giving people the benefit of the doubt. If you've been thinking of redecorating your space, buying new furniture, or painting, it's probably best to wait until Venus retrograde is over before you go for it.

Moon Cycles

Eclipse season is here! On the 14th, the lunar eclipse in Virgo is a call to adventure. Whatever about your life has felt unsatisfying, or like it's the wrong fit, may become unbearable now. This is your moment to make a change, even if it's scary.

Then on the 29th, the solar eclipse in Aries is an important one for you, likely to mark a new beginning in your private life. This could mean a change in your living situation, a transformation of your feelings, or a chance to learn more about your family.

Power Days

The 1st has the potential to be incredibly romantic: if you're planning a date, opt for cozy vibes over big thrills. Think outside the box on the 9th, when creative solutions are likely to be more successful than traditional ones. If you step outside your comfort zone on the 23rd, the universe will reward you!

Days to Watch For

Try to avoid clingy or demanding people on the 2nd: you need your space right now! On the 16th, insecurities may cause you to hang back at work, but don't let great opportunities pass you by just because you're scared. It's easy to accidentally hurt others' feelings on the 22nd, so speak with care!

April

Good news: Mercury retrograde ends on the 7th, and Venus retrograde ends on the 12th! After this, *no* planets are retrograde through the end of the month, making this an uncommonly good time to make big strides toward your goals. The Sun moves into Taurus on the 19th. While it's here, make a point of having fun and enjoying yourself! It's important to stop and smell the roses every once in a while. Don't let yourself get too busy to have fun.

Moon Cycles

The Libra Full Moon on the 12th shines a spotlight right on you! This is your opportunity to show off your skills to the world. Don't be modest right now: if you let people see what you're made of, amazing new opportunities will come your way.

There's a good chance a new relationship (or an exciting new friendship) will begin under the Taurus New Moon on the 27th. If you want to get to know somebody better, don't wait around for them to come to you—be assertive!

Power Days

Your intuition is like a superpower on the 5th: listen to it! Be generous with your time and energy on the 6th—especially with family members or elders—and you'll reap unexpected benefits. Your charm and popularity get a boost on the 20th: it's a great day to schedule dates, interviews, or social events.

Days to Watch For

On the 4th, you may be unusually sensitive to criticism from people in your life, so do your best not to take anything too personally. You may feel threatened at work on the 13th, but if you keep a cool head, you'll be just fine. Your judgment's a bit scrambled on the 18th: wait a day or two before making important decisions.

May

Mercury joins the Sun in Taurus on the 10th, making the time between the 10th and 20th some of the best days of the year for creative expression! Don't worry about being productive just now—relaxing, having fun, and doing what brings you joy are more likely to benefit you in the long run, anyway. Toward the end of the month, the Sun and Mercury both move into

Gemini (on the 20th and 25th, respectively). Pay attention to the small things, especially at work. Slow and steady wins the race right now.

Moon Cycles

The Scorpio Full Moon on the 12th may kick off a bit of drama in your friend group—especially involving gossip or secrets coming to light. Don't fan the flames! The more you can be a support for others right now, the better you'll feel.

On the 26th, the Gemini New Moon is a perfect opportunity to change up your daily routines. Don't worry about the big picture or your long-term goals just now: focus on what makes you feel happy and fulfilled in the moment.

Power Days

The 1st is an ideal day for asking someone out: you're confident and charming, and your good heart shines through. Don't be too rigid with your plans on the 17th: if a spur-of-the-moment opportunity comes your way, take it. Take the initiative on the 23rd! People will respond best to straightforwardness today.

Days to Watch For

You may have trouble expressing yourself clearly on the 2nd: it's not the best day for meetings, presentations, or negotiations, if you can avoid it. On the 15th, it's easy to read *way* too much into what other people say. Chances are you'll feel a little down on the 28th, so plan to do something nice for yourself.

June

This month, the focus is on relationships: romantic ones (especially if you're in a committed partnership), close friendships, and even business connections. Three planets move into Cancer this month: Mercury on the 8th, Jupiter on the 9th, and the Sun on the 20th. Especially between the 20th and 26th, invest in your connections with other people. As much as you can during these days, put your energy into collaborating on projects, working through differences, giving and receiving support, and simply enjoying each other's company.

Moon Cycles

The Sagittarius Full Moon on the 11th is a moment for necessary self-reflection. Forget about the hustle and bustle of life for a moment, and think about how your spirit is doing: What's going on in your inner world? What does your soul need to keep growing?

Then on the 25th, a New Moon in Cancer is one of the best days of the year for meeting new people who will end up being important in your life. This is a moment for reaching out and making connections, whether or not it's a romantic one.

Power Days

Treat yourself on the 12th! Buy something beautiful, get a new haircut, or take yourself out for a delicious meal. The 20th is a good day for small acts of kindness—both doing them for others and gracefully receiving them when others do them for you. The 24th is one of the best days for relationships all year, especially for beginning new ones.

Days to Watch For

It's easy to put others on a pedestal on the 4th, expecting that they can solve all your problems. Remind yourself that they're only human, just like you. Maintain some healthy skepticism on the 18th, especially if people or opportunities seem too good to be true. Treat yourself with extra gentleness on the 23rd: avoid scheduling anything taxing today.

July

Saturn retrograde begins this month on the 13th. If you've been working too hard lately or neglecting your personal life in favor of your ambitions, this is an important time to ease off the gas and make sure you're happy with the path you're on. Then the second of this year's three Mercury retrogrades begins on the 18th. Be extra careful about making assumptions about other people's desires, feelings, or mental state right now: don't try to read anyone's mind. Finally, Venus enters Cancer on the 30th: romance may enter your life in the month ahead!

Moon Cycles

On the 10th, the Full Moon in Capricorn invites you to assert yourself! Especially if you've felt overlooked or walked all over lately, this is a time for reminding the people in your life—and yourself—that *your* needs and feelings matter, too.

On the 24th, the New Moon in Leo creates the right conditions for deep, emotional conversations. Opening up about your feelings under this Moon—especially to a crush, a newer partner, or a friend who's recently entered your life—will pave the way for stronger relationships, increased intimacy, and greater trust.

Power Days

Emotions are intense on the 16th, but your judgment is solid: trust yourself. The 22nd is an ideal day for dating and socializing, when you're likely to attract exactly the energy you're looking for. Unexpected work opportunities may come your way on the 29th: even if they weren't part of your long-term plan, it might be worth taking the leap.

Days to Watch For

You're likely to feel irritated by other people, or just lonely, on the 1st: treat yourself with kindness and trust that this feeling will pass soon. Avoid scheduling dates (especially first dates!) on the 9th: it could be hard to connect right now. Disagreements with your family or roommates are likely on the 17th, so devote some time to smoothing things over.

August

With Venus in Cancer for most of the month (it leaves on the 25th), this is likely to be one of the most romantic months of the year for you—but only if you can let down your guard long enough to really connect! Approach people with an open mind and heart, and you may forge rich and lasting relationships. Mercury retrograde ends on the 11th, which means communication should go a *lot* more smoothly. If you've been waiting to bring up a delicate topic, you can go for it now.

Moon Cycles

If any money issues have been brewing, they're likely to come to a head under the Aquarius Full Moon on the 9th. This could be somewhat stressful in the moment—but it's just as likely to be something good! You may finally get that raise you've been working toward or receive an unexpected windfall.

Expect to feel a bit antsy under the Virgo New Moon on the 23rd. Everything in your life may suddenly seem so boring! It might be a passing mood—but if you *really* need a change, this is one of the best times to make it.

Power Days

The 8th is an ideal day to ask for a raise, apply for that dream job, or speak up in a meeting. The 11th is a great day for meeting someone new or taking a relationship to the next level: the conditions are right for romance. Trust your intuition on the 25th: your gut won't steer you wrong.

Days to Watch For

Insecurities could flare up on the 1st, so try to spend time with people who give your confidence a boost. Jealousy could be a problem on the 5th. Your partner (or someone else close to you) might seem to be distant or insensitive on the 18th, but trust that it isn't personal—it probably has nothing to do with you!

September

With Mercury and the Sun both moving into Libra this month (Mercury on the 18th, the Sun on the 22nd), the focus for you shifts to your work life—not just the day-to-day tasks, but your overall career. This is an ideal time for negotiating promotions or raises, creating or revising your five-year (or longer!) plan, or beginning to lay the groundwork for a career change. Mars also enters Scorpio on the 22nd: friends will help you reach your goals right now, so don't be shy about asking for support.

Moon Cycles

It's eclipse season again! Expect some turbulence under the lunar eclipse in Pisces on the 7th. Your daily activities are likely to be disrupted, so try not to be too rigid about your routines right now. Stay open to changing your plans—and your mind.

If last month's Virgo New Moon wasn't enough motivation for you to change your life, the solar eclipse in Virgo on the 21st will give you an extra push. You deserve a life that's exciting and fulfilling, and this eclipse opens the door for you to find it!

Power Days

Things should go smoothly for you on the 2nd: make the most of the good vibes by taking risks, meeting people, and having new experiences. The 16th is a perfect day for tackling tough issues and thorny emotions: you've got the strength and good judgment to handle anything. Unexpected professional opportunities may present themselves on the 23rd: trust that you've got what it takes to succeed.

Days to Watch For

People in your life may get extra bossy or nosy on the 3rd: be prepared to set (and uphold!) boundaries. On the 4th, you might be tempted to take on way more work than you can handle, so don't overcommit. Watch out for tension with coworkers on the 29th, and deal with things now so they don't get worse.

October

This month, Mercury and the Sun both move into Scorpio (Mercury on the 6th, the Sun on the 22nd). Between the 22nd and 29th, it's important to do things that bring you closer to your community. That could mean anything from volunteering, to chatting with neighbors when you take walks, to going out to socialize with your friends more. Basically, don't isolate yourself. Venus also enters Libra on the 13th: if you have somebody you've wanted to make a good impression on at work, this is your moment to shine.

Moon Cycles

Under the Aries Full Moon on the 6th, your job is to tend to your home life, whether that means spending time with the people you live with, dealing with any home maintenance project you've been putting off, or just spending a really nice night in.

Then on the 21st, the New Moon in Libra is one of the best days of the year for setting new career goals and putting new plans in motion. Have faith in yourself, dream big, and believe in your potential as you move forward!

Power Days

On the 14th, you may be drawn to people outside your usual type, so don't be scared to take a chance on somebody totally different. Schedule time for socializing on the 26th: the more friends you connect with, the better you'll feel today. Your confidence gets a boost on the 28th: ask for what you want, and you'll probably receive it!

Days to Watch For

Your personal life and professional life could pull you in different directions on the 13th, so focus on finding a balance that works for you. If you're not careful, overconfidence could get you in trouble on the 16th. Self-doubt may rear its head on the 20th, but helping others will help pull you out of any ruts.

November

The final Mercury retrograde of 2025 has arrived, lasting from the 9th to the 29th of this month, and spending time in Scorpio and Sagittarius. For you, this is likely to be a particularly reflective period, so don't pressure yourself to get a lot done. Mars, the Sun, and Venus all enter Sagittarius this month as well (on the 4th, 21st, and 30th, respectively). Even though this could be a busy time of year, with all these planets in your solar twelfth house of privacy and spirituality, try to get some alone time. You need (and deserve!) your rest.

Moon Cycles

On the 5th, the Full Moon in Taurus invites you to forget about your obligations for a moment and think about what actually brings you joy. There may be a lot of demands on your time, but you need (and deserve!) some space to enjoy yourself, too.

The Scorpio New Moon on the 20th is a perfect time to meet new people, gather with your friends, or join a new group. Trying to go it alone probably won't go well for you right now; leaning on your community is what will bring success.

Power Days

On the 8th, refill your cup by socializing and having fun with friends (it's an especially good day to throw a party!). Think outside the box on the 10th, and you can come up with amazing creative solutions to whatever problems you're facing. On the 15th, open up about your feelings: it'll feel amazing to get things off your chest.

Days to Watch For

Avoid making impulse purchases on the 2nd, especially expensive ones: you'll probably end up regretting it. You may feel compelled to make big life decisions on the 17th, but wait a few days before you commit—there's a good chance you'll change your mind. Don't hesitate to stand up for yourself if you feel disrespected on the 24th.

December

Finally, at the close of the year, the inner planets begin entering your home sign of Capricorn once more: Mars on the 15th, the Sun on the 21st, and Venus on the 24th. This is your time! You're confident, powerful, and ready to live life on your own terms. Especially between the 21st and the end of the month, the more you assert yourself, the happier you'll feel. Be mindful of others' feelings, but don't be scared to advocate for your needs, too.

Moon Cycles

On the 4th, the Full Moon in Gemini directs your focus to your health. Especially if there's something you've been worried about, this is an ideal time to take charge—whether by getting help, making changes to your life, or simply taking better care of your body.

You may find yourself feeling somewhat drained under the Sagittarius New Moon on the 19th. This is an important day for reflection, so do your best to schedule some quiet time alone. Everyone needs to rest and recharge sometimes, even someone as motivated as you!

Power Days

Your intuition is extra sensitive on the 7th: if you're picking up on a feeling, it's worth paying attention to. The 13th is a great day to go on a date, confess feelings to a crush, or strengthen an existing relationship by spending quality time together. Break out of your usual routine on the 22nd!

Days to Watch For

You're likely to feel indecisive on the 14th: don't let yourself be pressured to make any important decisions before you're ready! You're sensitive to other people's emotions on the 21st, but don't let someone else's bad mood become your problem. Relationships are likely to be stressful on the 27th, but it's almost definitely going to pass quickly.

Aquarius

The Water Bearer
January 20 to February 18

Element: Air
Ruling planets: Saturn (traditional) and Uranus (modern)
Keyword: Independence
Key phrase: I imagine

Gemstone: Amethyst
Power stones: Aquamarine, chrysocolla
Color: Electric blue
Flower: Orchid

All about Aquarius

Strengths and Gifts

The Sun enters Aquarius, the third and final air sign of the zodiac, in late January. A classic air sign, you're fun, engaging, and intellectual. You're also idealistic, future-oriented, and inventive: a true original. Some people are afraid to experiment or break the mold, but you, Aquarius, specialize in it!

Your creative, curious mind is one of the very best things about you. You love learning about the world, exploring new ideas, and asking *why*. It's endlessly satisfying to you to deepen your knowledge and gain a clearer understanding of how the universe works, and you take an intellectual interest in even the most complicated or far-out theories. While some people prefer to stick with tradition and do things the same way they've always been done, you're an innovator. You believe it's always possible to expand your knowledge and to find different and better ways of doing things.

This means that you tend to be right on the cutting edge, from fresh fashion trends to the latest technologies. You're quick to see the potential in new ideas—the more creative, experimental, or unique, the better. (If there's one sign that's most captivated by sci-fi, outer space, and the future, it's Aquarius!)

Your interest in breaking barriers gives you a rebellious streak. You're not someone who cares much about fitting in or doing what people expect. To you, the most important thing is following your own path and staying true to yourself, no matter what others may think. You aren't afraid to break with convention: from your career to your romantic relationships to your personal style, you do things the way *you* want, not the way you're "supposed" to.

You're especially willing to break the rules when those rules are limiting, intolerant, or unfair. You have a strong idealistic streak and a deep love for humanity, and you won't hesitate to stand up for the underdog. Whether that means marching in protests and picket lines, arguing for what you believe in, or simply showing up to help out in your community, you thrive when you know that you're making the world a better place.

Your unique personality and unconventional ideas can sometimes make others—particularly more traditional people—have a hard time understanding you! But you have a friendly charm that can win over just about anyone when you set your mind to it.

Friendship and Love

For you, Aquarius, friendship is one of the most beautiful parts of life! You're charming and popular (probably much more than you realize), and you find deep satisfaction in socializing, connecting with people, and having the sort of deep, philosophical conversations that last late into the night. Half the pleasure of coming up with new theories and ideas about life is discussing them with other people!

This means that you tend to be most drawn to people who are smart, unique, and creative like you. It doesn't mean you're looking for a carbon copy of yourself—that would be boring—only that it's important that you can connect with friends and partners on an intellectual level. From light banter to serious conversation, you need people around you who are on the same wavelength.

The most fulfilling romances for you, therefore, are often the ones that begin as friendship—or, at least, the ones where there's a strong friendship connection. You're probably not particularly interested in traditional romantic gestures—candlelit dinners, red roses, diamond rings, and so on—and may struggle to find common ground in relationships with people who *do* want these things. For you, a better date might be staying up all night talking at a dive bar, going to a modern art opening, or visiting a planetarium.

More than most, you may also be open to nontraditional arrangements. From open relationships to long-distance ones to deciding that marriage just isn't for you, there's no one way your love life has to look. Stay open to experimentation!

Just keep in mind that life isn't *all* about the mind. You have emotions, too! You may sometimes feel a bit detached from your emotional side, but it's important to learn to get in touch with it and to share your feelings every so often—*especially* with friends and partners. It may take you a bit of effort to express your love for them, or to express your needs and desires in the relationship, but it's worth it to try.

Work and Money

In order for you to truly be happy in your career, Aquarius, you need intellectual stimulation and a sense of purpose. If your brain isn't challenged, you'll get bored quickly—and if you don't feel like your work is doing anything to benefit humanity, you'll probably end up frustrated and burned out. You could excel in any number of fields, from academia (especially philosophy and the sciences) to the arts (especially architecture, experimental music, or performance art) to activism (especially dreaming up big actions or campaigns). You're likely to do best in workplaces that allow (even encourage!) you to let your individuality shine through.

You're probably not overly focused on money, buying flashy cars or a big house, or keeping up with the Joneses. As long as you have enough money to live a good and fulfilling life—whatever that means to *you*—you can be happy. With your interest in innovation and new tech, you probably have some interest—or at least curiosity—in crypto or NFTs. Just be careful to balance any investment in the more experimental side of things with a solid safety net, just in case.

Struggles and Growth

On the one hand, you're tremendously idealistic and forward-thinking. You love humanity, you value justice, and you aren't afraid to break with traditions that don't match up with your principles. Once you've made up your mind about something, though, your thinking can be a bit rigid. You think there are definite right and wrong answers about most things, and when loved ones' opinions differ from yours, you're not always inclined to hear them out. Try to remember that life is complicated, that two things can be true, and that even when others' ideas are different from yours, they still have value.

You also struggle sometimes to take care of—or even feel connected to—your body. You live so much in your mind that you can forget about the importance of eating, moving, and sleeping. Even more than that, you forget that your body can help you *enjoy* the world, too. If you take time to enjoy the physical world—from food to sex to the simple pleasure of a walk on a sunny day—it'll enrich your life more than you realize.

Journaling Page

Think about your goals for 2025. Which of your Aquarius gifts—intellect, unconventionality, inventiveness, idealism—will you call on to help you achieve them? Which elements of the Aquarius personality do you want to lean into this year?

The Year Ahead for Aquarius

The Eclipses

As you start planning for the year ahead, begin by looking at the eclipses. In 2025, we'll get four eclipses total—two in Virgo and one each in Aries and Pisces. Eclipses mark important beginnings, endings, and turning points. Sometimes their effects are so small that they're barely noticeable in the moment, while other times they're dramatic and undeniable. Your experience of each one will depend on what else is in your personal birth chart.

The first of the four 2025 eclipses is the lunar eclipse in Virgo on March 14th. Be prepared for some drama around money to arise for you. This could be stressful, like arguments with someone you share expenses with, but it could also be exciting, like an inheritance or unexpected gift.

Next up is the Aries solar eclipse on March 29th. You're likely to learn a lot right now, especially from (or about) the people in your orbit. Small details you pick up on under this eclipse may turn out to be significant down the road, so pay attention—even to things that seem unimportant right now.

The Pisces lunar eclipse on September 7th is likely to highlight financial issues in your life. You may experience stress or arguments about money, or accidentally spend way more than you intended to—but you may also come into unexpected cash, or receive something of major (but non-monetary) value to you.

The final eclipse of 2023 is the Virgo solar eclipse on September 21st. Back in March, the Virgo lunar eclipse may have stirred up issues around money (especially money or bills you share with others). Now, the Virgo solar eclipse shows you a new way to manage resources in a way that feels right and in tune with your values.

The Big Picture

Beyond the eclipses, you can find important info about your year ahead by watching the movement of the outer planets: Jupiter, Saturn, Uranus, Neptune, and Pluto. In contrast to the inner planets, which can tell you about your day-to-day life, these five outer planets have a lot to show you about the big picture, because they spend months (or often years!) at a time in the same sign.

First, look to **Jupiter**, planet of growth and good fortune, for clues about what kind of luck you'll have in the year ahead. Jupiter spends about half of 2025 in Gemini, then moves into Cancer on June 9th, where it'll stay for the rest of the year. While it's in Gemini, your romantic prospects look particularly good! And the more you open your heart and express your feelings, the better your luck will get. After Jupiter moves into Cancer, you can create good luck for yourself by being generous with your time, doing favors for others, and treating the details of your work with attention and care.

Next up is **Saturn**, planet of authority and discipline. This year, Saturn splits its time between Pisces and Aries. It starts out in Pisces, moves into Aries on May 24th, and returns to Pisces on September 1st. While it's in Pisces, you'll want to get serious about dealing with your finances. This is the time for building a strong foundation by getting back to the basics with budgeting and saving, rather than making big purchases or risky investments. While Saturn is in Aries, you may find yourself becoming judgmental with friends, neighbors, and people in your community. Focus on listening, understanding, and investing in strong relationships.

Neptune, planet of dreams and confusion, also splits its time between Pisces and Aries this year, starting the year in Pisces, entering Aries on March 30th, and returning to Pisces on October 22nd. During its time in Pisces, there's a good chance you'll be tempted to make risky financial decisions. You'll especially want to watch out for scams right now! Some risks are okay, but make sure you're getting solid outside advice. When Neptune enters Aries, any preconceived notions are likely to be challenged, especially by new friends or acquaintances. Don't be rigid: stay open to changing your mind.

Uranus, the most unpredictable of all the planets, spends much of 2025 in Taurus (though it dips into Gemini from July 7th through November 7th, then moves into Gemini for the long haul in early 2026). It's been in Taurus since 2018, so this is a continuation of a story that's been going on for a while now. For you, Uranus in Taurus has marked big changes in your home life, drama in your family, or even a big move. You've probably broken with some traditions as you've figured out how you can stay connected with your roots while still being *you*. Once Uranus enters Gemini, be prepared for excitement! This is likely to be a thrilling time for dating—it's also an ideal time to focus on your creativity by diving deeper into an artistic practice, or picking one up for the first time.

Finally, **Pluto**—the most distant and slowest-moving of the planets—continues its yearslong journey through Aquarius, where it'll be until 2043. With the planet of rebirth and transformation in your home sign, this is likely to be an intense but deeply meaningful time for you. (January 21st, when the Sun and Pluto align in your home sign of Aquarius, may be particularly dramatic.) You're overcoming old blockages, redefining yourself and your life, and gradually moving forward with new clarity and purpose.

Your Ruling Planet

You, Aquarius, have not one but *two* ruling planets: according to traditional astrology, you're ruled by disciplined Saturn, while modern astrology says your ruler is rebellious Uranus. Choose one—or pay attention to both! In 2025, Saturn has one retrograde period (from July 13th to November 27th), and Uranus has two (from the start of the year to January 30th, and from September 6th through the end of the year). During Saturn retrograde, expect to feel less motivated than usual. Use this time to reflect on your goals and values, and rearrange your responsibilities and obligations if they aren't working for you. When Uranus is retrograde, it's a good time to look at the world with clear eyes. You can sometimes be a rebel without a cause—so use these retrogrades to make sure you're doing something meaningful, not just lashing out! Outside of the periods when Uranus is retrograde, May 17th is an important day for this planet: Uranus aligns with the Sun that day, and you're likely to experience a major breakthrough or inspiration.

January

The year 2025 kicks off with three retrograde planets: Mars, Jupiter, and your ruling planet of Uranus. Mars retrograde in particular is likely to stir up relationship conflicts, especially before January 6th. The Sun moves into your home sign of Aquarius on the 19th—this is your season! Focus on yourself and your needs: by refilling your own cup now, you'll be better able to show up for others later on. When Mercury joins the Sun in Aquarius on the 27th, don't hesitate to express your own unique point of view.

Moon Cycles

The year gets started with a Full Moon in Cancer on the 13th. This Moon illuminates the small actions you can take to heal old wounds. You don't have to take dramatic action right now: making small changes to your daily life can make a huge difference.

Then on the 29th, the Aquarius New Moon is *your* Moon: this is one of the best opportunities all year to make a fresh start, finally start moving toward a longtime dream, or simply decide to believe in yourself. Dream big and take action!

Power Days

If you think outside the box on the 2nd, you'll be able to solve even the thorniest of problems. Friendships and relationships may feel extra deep on the 28th, and expressing your feelings honestly can make them even stronger. The 30th is likely to be an exceptionally lucky day, so take a (calculated) risk or two!

Days to Watch For

Bad feelings, *especially* jealousy, may be stronger than usual on the 14th. Feel your feelings, but try not to act on them today. Impulsive actions probably won't go well on the 15th, so avoid making important choices on the spur of the moment. Watch out for conflict with family or roommates on the 21st: avoid fanning the flames!

February

Mercury moves into Pisces on the 14th, followed by the Sun on the 18th. With both of these planets in your solar second house, it's important now to think about what you value in life—not just money or material things, but also your spiritual values. You'll probably find yourself having deep conversations (and possibly arguments!) about values with others in your life. Mars retrograde ends on the 23rd, and you're likely to find that most things in your life, but *especially* your duties at work, start to go more smoothly now.

Moon Cycles

On the 12th, the Leo Full Moon marks an important moment in one of your relationships—likely with a spouse, partner, or best friend. Maybe a long-simmering conflict is finally coming to a head, or maybe you need to confess your feelings! Communicate openly, and you'll connect on a new level.

Then on the 27th, the Pisces New Moon is an ideal time to commit (or recommit) to your values. Set new goals, rethink your five-year plan so that it aligns with your ideals, or simply take some time to *enjoy* your favorite parts of life.

Power Days

The 7th is a great day for flirting, spending quality time with your partner, or asking your crush out. Travel (whether you're going across town or across the world) is likely to be fun and rewarding on the 17th. Be assertive on the 19th! It'll get the results you want.

Days to Watch For

You may get frustrated by a family member's stubbornness on the 5th. Return to the problem in a day or two and it'll be easier to find common ground. The more rigidly you try to stick to your plans on the 11th, the more annoying the day will be. Your emotions might get a bit scrambled on the 12th!

March

Two important planetary retrogrades begin this month: Venus on the 1st and Mercury on the 15th. During Venus retrograde, you may feel a bit lonely or misunderstood in your social circle, especially before the 27th. If you're single, this probably won't be the best season for dating—but that doesn't mean it's impossible! During Mercury retrograde, expect some miscommunications with your friends, and do your best to treat everyone (including yourself) with a little extra patience. If you can, avoid making big financial decisions between the 29th and the end of Venus retrograde on April 12th.

Moon Cycles

Eclipse season is here! On the 14th, the lunar eclipse in Virgo is likely to feel particularly intense for you, activating deep thoughts and spurring intimate conversations with others. This is an opportunity to be transformed: whether you'll take it is up to you.

Two weeks later, on the 29th, the solar eclipse in Aries is likely to usher all kinds of fresh activity into your life! New projects, new studies, but most of all, new friends and acquaintances: this is a time to get excited about life in general.

Power Days

Spending time with the people you care about will be extra rewarding and sweet on the 10th. You can make *major* progress toward your goals on the 18th by putting in only a little extra time and effort. Your intuition is incredibly powerful on the 24th, so use it wisely!

Days to Watch For

You may feel lonely or misunderstood on the 9th, but trust that things are not as bad as they seem today. Ego conflicts are likely at work on the 17th: do your best not to get drawn into unnecessary power struggles! Your rebellious side could get you in trouble on the 26th: don't do anything *too* wild today.

April

Mercury and Venus retrograde both end this month (Mercury on the 7th, Venus on the 12th). After that, *no* planets are retrograde for the rest of the month. This is a relatively rare occurrence and a great opportunity to make moves and progress toward your goals. On the 18th, Mars moves into Leo. This could signal some conflict with someone close to you (especially a partner, spouse, or best friend), *or* it could mean that the two of you will work together toward a shared goal.

Moon Cycles

On the 12th, the Libra Full Moon brings sweetness, beauty, and change into your life. A chance encounter or surprising interaction might cause you to change all your plans. The best thing you can do right now is be open to taking risks!

Then on the 27th, the New Moon in Taurus is an ideal day to focus on your home life. Even the boldest adventurers deserve to feel safe and supported, so use this Moon to think about what you need to feel secure and happy.

Power Days

Trust your instincts on the 1st, even if you can't explain *why* you feel the way you do. The 7th is a beautiful day for trying something new in your neighborhood or city, especially with a partner or close friend. Your judgment is excellent on the 15th: it's a great day for setting goals, communicating boundaries, or making commitments.

Days to Watch For

Self-sabotage at work is a real risk on the 13th, so make sure you're not tearing yourself down today. You're likely to be irritable on the 20th—if you accidentally lash out at someone, don't be too proud to apologize! On the 23rd, you may feel smothered by a family member or old friend: set boundaries if you need to.

May

When Mercury moves into Taurus on the 10th, it's a perfect opportunity to delve deep into your own feelings and inner life. Deep conversations with parents or older relatives will be especially illuminating right now. It's also a good time to start (or restart) seeing a therapist. The Sun moves into Gemini on the 20th, followed by Mercury on the 25th. The best thing you can do for yourself right now is *have fun*. Relaxing, socializing, and getting out with your friends will enrich your life and your spirit tremendously.

Moon Cycles

On the 12th, the Full Moon in Scorpio is likely to mark a big professional moment for you. If you feel like you're suddenly in the spotlight, that's because you are! Your hard work is paying off, and people are noticing. Take advantage of any opportunities that arise because of this.

Then on the 26th, the New Moon in Gemini is one of the best days possible for beginning creative projects. Even if you're only in the brainstorming phase, your mind is filled with ideas, your imagination is sparkling, and you're embarking on something exciting and new.

Power Days

The 3rd is an exceptional day for falling in love, making a move, or bonding with your partner. If you've been feeling dissatisfied with your life, the 17th offers you an opportunity to make a move: even somewhat impulsive changes are likely to work out. On the 18th, act according to your values and it'll pay off in the long run.

Days to Watch For

Simmering tension with people close to you might erupt on the 4th: commit to dealing with things now! Your needs are likely to clash with your partner's on the 10th: honest, open-minded communication will help. The 19th probably isn't the best day for delicate conversations, so wait a day or two for best results.

June

When Venus moves into Taurus on the 6th, it's one of the best moments of the year for any home redecorating projects. June is also an ideal time to tend to your physical health, as Mercury, Jupiter, and the Sun all move into Cancer (on the 8th, 9th, and 20th, respectively). The more you care for your body right now—especially by making sure you're getting enough rest—the better everything else in your life will flow. Finally, Mercury enters Leo on the 26th: this is an ideal time for negotiations, both personal and professional.

Moon Cycles

The Sagittarius Full Moon on the 11th is probably going to be a very busy time, with lots of social engagements. It's possible you'll see (or even be part of) some drama in your friend group, but don't isolate yourself.

On the 25th, the New Moon in Cancer is an opportunity for you to simplify your life. Especially if you've taken on more than your fair share of caretaking or household tasks lately, this is a chance to rebalance things and move forward in a more equitable way.

Power Days

Be bold on the 1st! Today, the most direct approach (in both work and love) is likely to be the most productive one. Schedule difficult tasks and conversations for the 16th, and they'll probably turn out better than you hoped. The 27th is an ideal day for making difficult decisions.

Days to Watch For

Romantic insecurities may pop up on the 7th: if you're feeling bad about yourself today, don't worry too much, because the feeling should pass soon. Your temper may be a bit unpredictable on the 9th, but lashing out could cause bigger problems. Expect to make some mistakes on the 15th, and remember that it's not the end of the world!

July

Three planetary retrogrades begin this month: Neptune, Saturn, and Mercury. Mercury retrograde, which lasts from the 18th to August 11th, is likely to be the most disruptive of these. For you, it could manifest in missed connections or arguments in your close relationships. The key is not to try to read minds: if you want to know what's going on in someone's head, *ask them*. It's also not an ideal time for negotiating or signing contracts. If it's unavoidable, don't worry! Just make sure to read through everything extra carefully and get outside advice.

Moon Cycles

On the 10th, the Full Moon in Capricorn brings all your emotions to the surface, especially any you've been repressing or avoiding. Schedule some downtime today if you can. You'll do best if you can rest and take it easy right now.

Then on the 24th, the New Moon in Leo marks a good time to start new relationships, reach out to a crush, or make a commitment to someone. This is also a good day to negotiate; it's possible to work out a solution that makes *everyone* happy.

Power Days

The 4th should bring some lovely new energy into your life: in order to take advantage of it, just keep an open mind. Chances are good that you'll meet someone new and exciting on the 11th. The 24th is a better day for work than for play—and the harder you work, the more you'll be rewarded.

Days to Watch For

It may be hard to figure out what you really want or need on the 6th, so don't make any drastic changes to your life just now. On the 13th, your own ego may get in the way of success: listen to alternative perspectives. Expect some stress—especially in your relationships—on the 25th, and trust that by working through this, you're getting stronger.

August

Mars enters Libra on the 6th, and from now (especially after the 11th) until September 22nd, it's probably an excellent time for travel. It'll be especially rewarding to visit somewhere you've never been before. Mercury retrograde ends on the 11th: if you've had conflicts with people close to you, now is the time to patch things up. Venus enters Leo on the 25th, making this one of the best times of the year for love, whether you're starting a new relationship or strengthening an existing one.

Moon Cycles

Under the Aquarius Full Moon on the 9th, it's important to express your needs and emotions, especially if you've felt overlooked lately or if you've been putting others ahead of yourself. You matter, too! Right now, the best way to get what you need is to assert yourself.

You might feel like you can practically see into your loved ones' souls under the Virgo New Moon on the 23rd. Don't let this moment of deep understanding and intimacy go to waste! Use it as a chance to connect and get closer.

Power Days

If you advocate for yourself on the 7th, your life will improve immeasurably. The 15th is a great day for love (romantic *and* platonic) and simply enjoying the company of others. If there's something you've been nervous to do—asking someone out, taking a solo trip, initiating a tough conversation—go for it on the 17th.

Days to Watch For

Expect disagreements, especially with bosses or colleagues, on the 1st: focus on restoring the peace, not coming out the "winner." Overthinking is *not* your friend, especially on the 8th. If you're having trouble seeing an issue clearly, get advice from a friend. You may feel pulled in different directions on the 14th: try your best to stay true to yourself.

September

Mercury joins the Sun in Virgo on the 2nd, marking a time of deep conversations, intimate encounters, and serious thinking. You'll probably be unsatisfied with surface-level interactions right now: better to go deep. Most important for you, perhaps, is that Mars enters Scorpio on the 22nd, activating your confidence, your ambition, and your sheer will to achieve. This is a great time to start new projects, apply for new jobs, or negotiate for the promotion you've wanted (just be careful not to trample others in the process!).

Moon Cycles

The year's second eclipse season is here! On the 7th, the lunar eclipse in Pisces could mark a big financial shift for you. Unexpected windfalls are possible now, but the most important thing for you to do is to appreciate what you already have.

Then on the 21st, the solar eclipse in Virgo rehashes some of last month's themes, but in an even more pronounced way. Sometimes true intimacy is stressful, but that doesn't mean it's not worth it: let yourself get truly close to others.

Power Days

Follow your instincts on the 4th, even (or especially) when they lead you in unexpected directions. Don't shy away from deep conversations or uncomfortable topics on the 11th: this is a chance to truly build intimacy. Ask for your friends to support you on the 26th, especially if you've been having a tough time lately.

Days to Watch For

It could be easy to get drawn into unsatisfying relationships on the 5th: don't feel obligated to spend time with anyone unless you really want to! Others (especially family members) may pry into your life on the 10th: be serious about your boundaries. Do your best to avoid getting drawn into power struggles on the 24th.

October

There's some exciting career-focused energy in the air for you this month, as Mercury and the Sun join Mars in Scorpio (on the 6th and 22nd, respectively). Especially if you've been working hard toward a goal this year, there's a good chance you'll receive good news or start to see results now. Setting new career goals, networking (especially with people who are where you'd *like* to be one day), or simply working hard on your passion projects will all help you make the most of this time.

Moon Cycles

On the 6th, the Aries Full Moon could have you feeling a little stressed with all that you have to do! Plan for lots of errands and unexpected tasks to pop up, and just do the best you can with them. Trust that the busy feeling won't last forever!

On the 21st, a New Moon in Libra gives you the urge to expand your horizons by trying something new: taking a trip, starting a new course of study, stretching your limits. Pay attention to this feeling, and let it guide you.

Power Days

On the 1st, surprises that seem stressful at first might turn out to be *exactly* what you needed, so stay open! You're likely to meet someone special on the 14th, especially if you step outside of your daily routines. Your mind is incredibly sharp on the 19th: it's a day for decision-making, debating, and checking tasks off your to-do list.

Days to Watch For

Stress at work may lead to mistakes on the 2nd, but if you *slow down*, you'll be fine. You may feel defensive on the 7th, but try not to take it out on others—it'll only make things worse for you, too. The 15th isn't a good day to take big risks or drastic action—hold off a day or two!

November

The third and final Mercury retrograde of the year is here, lasting from the 9th to the 29th. Between the 11th and 18th, you may experience some misunderstandings or friction in your social circle, community, or a club or group you belong to. Talk things through and don't assume the worst of others! From the 18th through the 29th, avoid scheduling important work meetings, presentations, or job interviews if you can. If that's not possible, give yourself extra time to prepare, and you should be fine.

Moon Cycles

The Taurus Full Moon on the 5th is a big one for you. Expect to be called to focus on your home life: a maintenance project, a family drama, or a move to a new house or apartment could all demand your attention right now.

After you've dealt with that, the Scorpio New Moon on the 20th is a time to move your focus to your career, reputation, and public-facing life in general. Promotions, new job offers (especially if you've been looking to make a career change), or even awards are all possible under this Moon!

Power Days

By advocating for others—whether at work, in your community, or in your family—on the 3rd, you'll end up improving your own well-being, too. Take the initiative on the 10th, especially when it comes to planning group activities. The 16th is a beautiful day for getting things done and putting your energy to good use: don't let it go to waste!

Days to Watch For

Relationships (of all kinds) could get complicated on the 7th:
make an effort to stay kind and fair-minded, no matter how
frustrated you get. Tension with people close to you is almost
inevitable on the 11th: don't ignore the problem, but instead face
it head-on. Life's likely to feel a bit chaotic on the 21st—just go
with it!

December

The first half of December is likely to be fun and sociable for
you! As the month begins, the Sun, Venus, and Mars are all in
Sagittarius, and Mercury joins them on the 11th. It's a great
time for group activities. Then, in the second half of the month,
things take a more introspective turn as the planets begin moving into Capricorn: Mars on the 15th, the Sun on the 21st, and
Venus on the 24th. Take some time to reflect on the year and
what you want for the year ahead.

Moon Cycles

The Gemini Full Moon on the 4th may be one of the most exciting and romantic days of the year for you! Creative projects may
reach completion, crushes might confess their love, or you could
experience a breakthrough in your own understanding of yourself and your life.

Finally, on the 19th, the New Moon in Sagittarius is a perfect moment for making friends, joining groups, or connecting with your community. Especially if you've felt lonely lately, this is your chance to be reminded how many wonderful people are out there.

Power Days

On the 9th, seize the day! Don't wait for the perfect moment to go after what you want—do it now. The 16th is a great day for balancing work and play: you can have it all! On the 29th, you can find real clarity about what you want: trust yourself to know what's right for you.

Days to Watch For

Don't take your moods *too* seriously on the 7th: right now, your feelings are strong but not necessarily accurate. Energies are probably scattered on the 10th, so avoid scheduling serious, focused work for today if you can. Likewise, you can expect yourself to be easily distracted on the 24th.

$\mathcal{H}$

Pisces

The Fish
February 18 to March 20

Element: Water
Ruling planet: Jupiter (traditional) and Neptune (modern)
Keyword: Intuition
Key phrase: I dream

Gemstone: Aquamarine
Power stones: Jade, tourmaline
Color: Sea green
Flower: Water lily

All about Pisces

Strengths and Gifts

The Sun enters Pisces, the twelfth and final sign of the zodiac, in late March. As the final sign of the astrological year, Pisces, you hold some of the wisdom and experience of every sign that came before. You're dreamy, perceptive, and probably a bit spiritual, driven by creativity and compassion.

As a water sign, you're comfortable swimming through the sea of emotions. While some of your friends (especially the earth signs!) may prefer solid facts and figures, you understand that when it comes to human beings, things are rarely so cut-and-dried. You don't need data to guide you: your instincts and feelings almost never steer you wrong.

You're good at sensing what's going on beneath the surface with others. If a friend is stressed or sad (or excited or in love!), you can pick up on it even if they don't say anything. Other people's emotions tend to affect you deeply, and you're sensitive to the energies in a room. (There's a good chance you're at least a little bit psychic, Pisces!)

Because of all this, you feel uncommonly connected to other people and to humanity at large. You have an innate understanding of the ways we're all interdependent, and the ways our joys, struggles, and feelings are bound together. This makes you one of the most compassionate, least selfish signs in the zodiac. It's rare that you'll act out of selfish motives: you care about *everybody's* happiness, not just your own, and you want to transcend the boundaries that keep us divided from one another.

Whether or not you participate in any organized religion, you probably have a deep spiritual side and a need to connect with something larger than yourself. In order to really be happy, what you need most isn't success, acclaim, or even love, but a feeling that you're aligned with your higher purpose.

You probably also have an artistic temperament and need a creative outlet to express—even to make sense of—the full depth and richness of your feelings. Whether you're a painter, a poet, a dancer, or simply someone who needs to journal each morning, tapping into your creative side helps you feel clear-headed, grounded, and able to take on the world.

Friendship and Love

You love love in all its forms. From friendships to romances to family ties and beyond, you value care and connection in your life. And with your sensitive, loving, and deeply compassionate nature, the people around you value *you* in return. Anyone would be lucky to have someone like you in their life, Pisces!

In your friendships, you're open-minded and compassionate. People know they can come to you for a shoulder to cry on, a sounding board, or a sympathetic ear. You have a strong understanding of emotions and relationships, and you give *great* advice. You love performing acts of kindness for your friends and can be counted on to know just what someone needs when they're having a hard time.

In your romantic relationships, you're searching for connection on a deeper, even spiritual level. To you, the ideal connection would be one that feels fated, or like you knew each other in a past life. You love chance meetings, weird coincidences, and encounters that feel written in the stars. No matter how realistic you try to be, or how tough you seem on the outside, there's a part of you that truly, deeply believes in the magic of true love. You want to feel swept away by a love that is dreamy, deep, and much bigger than yourself.

This can mean that, especially when you meet someone you feel a connection with, you're not always the most critical! While you give amazing advice to your friends and are incredible at helping them spot potential red flags, you don't always notice them when they pop up in your own life and relationships. (On the flip side, it can mean that you get *incredibly* sensitive, even hurt, when a crush or partner makes even a tiny mistake or simply reveals that they're only human.)

For you, Pisces, the key is to remember that it's necessary to maintain boundaries in your relationships. While there's a part of you that's looking for perfect, unconditional, boundaryless love, all real-life relationships rely on communication, give-and-take, and healthy boundaries.

Work and Money

You're probably more interested in the spiritual side of life than the practical side, Pisces—which means you're unlikely to thrive in work environments that are too rigid, structured, or businesslike. While all jobs require *some* practical elements, you may find it hard to be happy in settings where the bottom line is the primary focus. Instead, any work that involves spirituality—from minister to psychic to meditation teacher and beyond—could be fulfilling for you. Likewise, work that taps into your compassion, creativity, and ability to connect with people—from counselor or teacher to public speaker or musician—is likely to highlight your gifts and lead to success.

If you could have things your way, you'd never think about money at all: from art to love to the cosmos, there are so many things you'd *much* rather spend your time thinking about. It can be a little tempting for you to bury your head in the sand and wait for a windfall or hope that the finances will just work themselves out; but since dealing with this stuff is unavoidable, asking friends or a partner for support may be a big help.

Struggles and Growth

You tend to go through life with your head in the clouds—which isn't a bad thing! The world would probably be a better place if more people dreamed a bit more. But this might make you a bit absent-minded, showing up late to appointments or forgetting to do things you said you would. Remember that this affects people beyond just you, and try to avoid committing to tasks or projects that you don't realistically think you'll get to.

You're one of the most loving, compassionate signs in the zodiac, Pisces. You accept people for who they are, and when a friend needs you, you're there. Sometimes, though, you give so much, while asking for so little, that you end up resenting the people in your life. You can avoid feeling this way by advocating for yourself and respecting your own limits *before* things get to this point. Whether that means having a hard talk with someone who tends to walk all over you, asking for more support and care from your friends, or simply saying *no* once in a while, it'll make your relationships—and *you*—stronger.

Journaling Page

Think about your goals for 2025. Which of your Pisces gifts—perceptiveness, wisdom, compassion, creativity—will you call on to help you achieve them? Which elements of the Pisces personality do you want to lean into this year?

The Year Ahead for Pisces

The Eclipses

To get a sense of the storyline of your year ahead, it's smart to begin by looking at the eclipses. Each year has them, and they mark important moments in the year: beginnings, endings, or moments of transition and change. Like most years, 2025 has four of them: two in Virgo and one each in Aries and Pisces. For you, the eclipses in Virgo and Pisces are likely to be especially profound—but it's worth paying attention to all four!

First up is the lunar eclipse in Virgo on March 14th. For you, this one is all about your close relationships. If you've been nursing a crush or involved in a will-they-or-won't-they type of flirtation, this eclipse is likely to bring clarity! If you're in a committed relationship, any long-simmering frustrations or disagreements will demand to be dealt with now.

Two weeks later, the solar eclipse in fiery Aries on March 29th marks a fresh start for you—especially in terms of your finances. If you want to make more money, if you need to get serious about budgeting, or if you simply want to be better about actually using your money to *enjoy* your life, this is your moment to turn over a new leaf.

The lunar eclipse in Pisces arrives on September 7th, and it's likely to be an especially potent one for you, Pisces. Expect big revelations in your personal life, shifts in your self-image,

♓

or even urges to act out. If you need a change in your life, this eclipse will let you know—and will show you what you can do about it.

Finally, the Virgo solar eclipse falls on September 21st, and like the Virgo lunar eclipse back in March, it's likely to mark an important turning point in your relationships. Specifically, it's a moment to take all that you've learned—about yourself *and* others—this year to find a way forward that works for everyone.

The Big Picture

Beyond the eclipses, it's helpful to take a look at the movement of the outer planets of Jupiter, Saturn, Uranus, Neptune, and Pluto. These five planets are the farthest from the Sun, so they move more slowly through the zodiac, spending months (and often years!) at a time in the same sign. Unlike the inner planets, which provide a good map of your moods and daily life, the outer planets are best at teaching you about the big picture of your year ahead.

First up is **Jupiter**, planet of expansiveness and abundance—and for you, Pisces, one of your two ruling planets! It spends roughly half the year in Gemini, then moves into Cancer on June 9th for the rest of the year. While Jupiter is in Gemini, focus on your home life. It's a great time to reconnect with family, look for a new house or apartment, or commit to putting down roots in the place where you live. Once Jupiter enters Cancer, the focus shifts to romance! Especially if you think of yourself as unlucky in love, things are likely to shift for you now. Make the most of it by putting yourself out there and expressing your feelings openly.

Next comes **Saturn**, planet of responsibility and discipline, which splits its time in 2025 between your home sign of Pisces and Aries. It starts the year in Pisces, moves into Aries on May 24th, and returns to Pisces on September 1st. While it's in Pisces, the best thing you can do is get serious about your relationship with yourself: it's an ideal time for unlearning old patterns, developing new ones, and generally taking responsibility for your own life and happiness. While Saturn is in Aries, focus on your finances! This is a time to get serious about what you need, on a practical level, to live the kind of life you want.

Neptune, planet of dreams and illusions, also splits its time between Pisces and Aries this year, starting the year in Pisces, entering Aries on March 30th, and returning to Pisces on October 22nd. While it's in Pisces, you might experience some confusion around your identity! This is a period for getting to know yourself better, and giving yourself permission to change or update your self-perception. Then when Neptune enters Aries, you may be tempted to make risky investments or get involved in other people's schemes. Be smart, and get outside advice before doing anything reckless right now!

Uranus, the most unpredictable of all the planets, spends much of 2025 in Taurus (though it dips into Gemini from July 7th through November 7th, then moves into Gemini for the long haul in early 2026). It's been in Taurus since 2018, so this is a continuation of a story that's been going on for a while now. For you, Uranus in Taurus has been a time to look at your daily routines and relationships through a new lens. Life has probably been extra hectic during these years—but you've learned a lot. Once Uranus enters Gemini, it becomes time to reevaluate your relationship to home, family, and tradition. Get ready to rebel against tradition, Pisces!

Finally, **Pluto**—the most distant and slowest-moving of the planets—continues its yearslong journey through Aquarius, where it'll be until 2043. This year, count on Pluto to bring long-buried secrets to light. In particular, you'll be called on to confront buried elements of your own psyche. Dig deep and be brave, and the truth will set you free!

Your Ruling Planet

You, Pisces, have not one but *two* ruling planets. According to traditional astrology, you're ruled by generous Jupiter; according to modern astrology, your ruler is dreamy Neptune. Choose one—or pay attention to both! Jupiter has two retrograde periods in 2025 (from the beginning of the year to February 4th, and from November 11th through the end of the year). Jupiter retrograde tends to be relatively gentle—and is often even a positive experience! These periods are times to introspect: focus on inner growth, not outer achievement. Neptune is retrograde from July 4th to December 10th, and you can expect to be especially clearheaded during this time—no wishful thinking or rose-colored glasses, just a hard and realistic look at the world. In contrast, June 23rd and December 20th are likely to be some of your *least* clearheaded days of the year! Confusion, insecurities, and even a little paranoia are likely on these days, so avoid making big decisions or scheduling important events on them if possible.

♓

January

The year 2025 begins with three retrograde planets: Mars, Jupiter, and Uranus. (It also begins with both Saturn and Neptune in your home sign of Pisces!) Mars retrograde may cause you to feel pressured to rush through your work or skimp on important details, especially before the 6th. Resist the urge to hurry! Take your time. Venus enters Pisces on the 2nd, marking a wonderful period of love—both for the people around you and also for yourself. People are attracted to you, and your relationships flow relatively easy. Luxuriate in this feeling!

Moon Cycles

On January 13th, the Cancer Full Moon gets the year started on a romantic note. Your heart is bursting—with love, creativity, or just passion for life—and the more you express your feelings under this Moon, the more happiness and fulfillment you'll attract.

Then on the 29th, the Aquarius New Moon is an important day for you to rest and recharge. In order to dream big, change the world, or simply live the life *you* want, you need energy! So right now, take some time to refill your cup.

Power Days

On the 4th, turn to your friends for help in dealing with difficult emotional situations: now is your chance to get through it. Things overall should go smoothly on the 18th, and it's a good day for introducing a new partner to your friends. Bold moves on the 24th, especially at work, could transform your life for the better.

Days to Watch For

The 10th is probably not the best moment for dating or asking someone out—try to wait a day or two at least. Romantic insecurity is likely on the 17th, so make a point of spending time with friends who make you feel good about yourself. Your ego is likely to take a hit on the 25th, but you can grow from this.

February

Venus leaves Pisces to enter Aries on the 4th, but don't worry— your season isn't over yet! Mercury enters Pisces on the 14th, and the Sun follows on the 18th. This makes February an ideal time to focus on *you*. You sometimes give so much of your love and care to others that you end up spreading yourself too thin. Right now, you have a perfect opportunity to recharge. Mars retrograde ends on the 23rd: if you've been feeling awkward or unmotivated, that changes now!

Moon Cycles

On the 12th, the Leo Full Moon invites you to take yourself a bit more seriously. You deserve happiness! And right now, small

♓

changes to your habits and routines—especially quitting things or people that aren't good for you—will pay off in a big way.

Then on the 27th, the Pisces New Moon is an opportunity to focus on *you*. You're deeply compassionate and tuned in to other people's feelings—but right now, it's important to think about what *you* want. It isn't selfish to treat your own life with care!

Power Days

On the 7th, spending some time alone (or with your inner circle) will give you some much-needed perspective and insight. You can do virtually anything you put your mind to on the 9th: make the most of today's motivated energy. The 23rd is a perfect day for socializing, so put something fun on the calendar.

Days to Watch For

Watch out not to overdo things on the 13th: enjoy the good energy today, but remember your limits! On the 20th, tensions with colleagues are likely to boil over unless you make a point of mending fences. You're likely to feel a bit blue on the 21st, but trust that things will start looking up soon.

March

Two important planetary retrogrades begin this month: Venus on the 1st and Mercury on the 15th. Venus retrograde is unlikely to be a great time for romance or dating (though anything is possible!), and it's best to avoid big purchases and changes to your look (like dramatic haircuts or new tattoos) during this period. (On the bright side, Venus returns to Pisces on the 27th to give you another shot at radical self-love!) During Mercury retrograde, especially until the 29th, try to avoid big financial transactions and contracts. Wait until next month if possible.

Moon Cycles

Eclipse season is here! On the 14th, the lunar eclipse in Virgo may bring about major changes in your relationships. Big differences with your partner may be highlighted. It's up to you to work through them—but if you do, you'll come out of this eclipse closer than you've ever been.

Then on the 29th, the solar eclipse in Aries invites you to make a fresh start in your financial life. You may get a windfall right now, an exciting new opportunity, or a big non-monetary gift. Whatever happens, make sure you're staying true to your deeper values.

Power Days

On the 4th, you have the good judgment and strong foundations to take smart risks: don't be scared to bet on yourself. Your confidence gets a boost on the 7th, so get out there and fight for what you want. Your intuition is like a superpower on the 19th: trust it!

♓

Days to Watch For

Your optimism might end up misleading you on the 2nd: before you do anything rash, get a second opinion from a family member or trusted friend. Everything, but especially your home life, is likely to seem worse than it really is on the 6th. You may get lonely on the 13th, so be extra gentle with yourself.

April

Both of the retrogrades that began in March end this month! Mercury stations direct on the 7th, followed by Venus on the 12th. If you've been holding off on making a big purchase, initiating a tricky conversation, or asking your crush out, the end of this month is a great time to go for it. (In fact, after the 12th, *no* planets are retrograde for the rest of the month, making this an ideal time to make moves.) And when the Sun enters Taurus on the 19th, expect your social calendar to fill up fast!

Moon Cycles

Under the Libra Full Moon on the 12th, you have the chance to rebalance your relationships. This is an ideal time for apologies (giving them *or* demanding them), paying off debts, and settling old scores so you can move forward in a better, fairer way.

Then the Taurus New Moon on the 27th is a chance to deepen your understanding of your neighborhood and daily life. It's an excellent time to start new community projects, plan future gatherings, or meet new people. (If you don't know your neighbors, this is an ideal time to connect.)

Power Days

The 2nd is a great day to schedule first dates, interviews, or any activity where it's important to make a good first impression. The 6th is one of the best days possible for starting creative projects. Chance encounters are likely on the 24th: don't lose your head, but don't be scared to deviate from the plan if something better comes along.

Days to Watch For

Self-doubt may flare up on the 3rd, so try to avoid situations and people that tend to make you feel worse about yourself. On the 10th, any differences or conflicts between you and your partner are likely to be heightened. You probably won't be especially motivated on the 17th, so avoid scheduling difficult tasks today.

May

Your home life is in the spotlight when the Sun and Mercury enter Gemini this month (on the 20th and 25th, respectively). This is a time for nesting: you might feel called to tend to your living space by tidying and reorganizing, initiate overdue discussions about dividing up the chores, or simply spend lots of time

♓

at home. It's also a great time to focus on family ties: conversations with parents, siblings, or other relatives will be especially deep right now. You can learn a *lot* about yourself by learning about your family.

Moon Cycles

On the 12th, the Scorpio Full Moon activates your courageous side. You may feel the urge now to take risks, to change your life, to bet on yourself in a big way. Don't lose your head completely—but don't hold back, either.

Then on the 26th, the Gemini New Moon invites you to open up about your feelings! You don't always like talking about your own emotions—you'd rather listen to others—but deep conversations right now, whether with a friend, family member, or therapist, can lead to important new beginnings.

Power Days

You can probably trust your first impressions about people on the 13th, especially in the context of your job. The 22nd is a good day for taking care of business: you can get a *lot* done if you put your mind to it. Conversations about your house, living space, or family history may reveal important information on the 29th.

Days to Watch For

Relationships are likely to feel just a little *off* on the 5th, but chances are good that it's just a passing feeling. It's hard to get close to people on the 7th, so it's probably not the best day for scheduling dates. Be careful not to take your own stress out on others on the 15th.

June

If you're looking for romance, Pisces, there's a strong chance you'll find it in June! Mercury, Jupiter, and the Sun all move into Cancer (on the 8th, 9th, and 20th, respectively), making it a perfect opportunity for you to get out, socialize, and have fun—and maybe meet someone special in the process. The more you put yourself out there, the more likely something magical will happen. When Mars enters Virgo on the 17th, you might experience some conflict in your close relationships. This isn't a bad thing! Talking it out now will make you stronger overall.

Moon Cycles

The Full Moon in Sagittarius on the 11th may thrust you into the spotlight, like it or not! This is your chance to show everyone what you're made of, or even to brag a little bit. Don't hide from the attention right now—you deserve to be proud!

♓

On the 25th, the New Moon in Cancer invites you to rebuild your confidence by doing whatever makes you happiest: trust your instincts! Right now, if you focus on listening to your heart and pleasing *yourself*, instead of other people, you won't go wrong.

Power Days

You're even more charming and likable than usual on the 16th: it's a good day for asking for what you need, because people should be happy to help out. Don't sit at home alone on the 17th if possible: it's a beautiful day for socializing. You're extra brave on the 29th, so make the most of it!

Days to Watch For

Arguments with a partner are likely on the 2nd (especially about issues related to housework or shared space), so take the time to talk it through. It's easy to overcommit on the 4th: be careful not to take on more than you can handle. Your temper could flare easily on the 18th: try not to take it out on the people you love!

July

Three planets station retrograde this month: Neptune, Saturn, and Mercury (on the 4th, 13th, and 18th, respectively). Of these three, Mercury retrograde is the one you're most likely to notice in your daily life—specifically, for you, in the form of disruptions to your daily habits and routines. This isn't necessarily a bad thing, as long as you stay flexible. Venus and Uranus both move into Gemini this month (on the 4th and 7th, respectively). Expect changes—probably lovely ones!—to your living situation. The more you can be open to surprises, the more you'll be able to take advantage of opportunities that arise.

Moon Cycles

The Capricorn Full Moon on the 10th is a time to support your friends—and to let them support *you*, too. If there's a project, question, or relationship you've been struggling with, your friends can give great advice and lighten your load today.

On the 24th, a New Moon in Leo is a good day for working hard, especially on projects you hope will lead to recognition or acclaim in the future. By handling the small stuff now, you'll be making huge strides toward your future goals.

Power Days

If you're single, there's a good chance you'll meet someone wonderful on the 1st, but they probably won't be your usual type. The 6th is the day to finally do the tasks you've been putting off: they won't be that bad. The 15th is a great day for romance, and dates at concerts or art museums should go especially well.

♓

Days to Watch For

If you rush through your work on the 7th, you could make major mistakes, so slow down and take the time you need. Mood swings could cause problems in your relationships on the 14th: don't pick fights today! You may feel bored with your life or relationships on the 26th, but wait a few days before you take action.

August

Mars enters Libra on the 6th. While it's here, watch out for passive-aggressiveness, both in yourself and the people around you. Better to be direct, even if it's hard! Then Mercury retrograde ends on the 11th, and all the disruptions and small irritations of the past few weeks should fade away now. Finally, relationships (of all kinds, not just romantic ones) become incredibly important for you when the Sun enters Virgo on the 22nd. Don't worry about being self-sufficient right now—ask for help when you need it.

Moon Cycles

The Full Moon in Aquarius on the 9th will probably be a highly emotional one for you. Questions, self-doubts, and even regrets might pop up right now. Care for yourself by scheduling some downtime to be alone, think, and rest.

On the 23rd, the New Moon in Virgo is a perfect moment for starting new relationships—or for resetting the terms of an existing relationship. If you've felt unsupported or overlooked lately, this is your chance to (gently, kindly!) let the other person know.

Power Days

You may get good financial news on the 3rd, and you also have the solid judgment to make good choices about your money today. The 11th is a lucky day to ask for favors, support, or even a raise. Trust your instincts on the 16th; your subconscious knows things your conscious mind doesn't.

Days to Watch For

Work responsibilities and personal obligations may clash on the 5th: the best thing you can do is prioritize and stay true to your values. The 10th is likely to be a bit dramatic, especially with family or roommates. Focus on not escalating things further. Expect the unexpected on the 24th, and know that any plans for today are likely to change.

September

The focus on relationships continues in September, as Mercury joins the Sun in Virgo on the 2nd. If you're struggling to solve a problem on your own, the best thing you can do is talk it over with someone you trust. On the 19th, Venus enters Virgo as well, and all your relationships—romantic and platonic alike—are likely to benefit. It's an ideal time for making a new love connection, but it's just as good for strengthening existing bonds and repairing fractured relationships.

Moon Cycles

Eclipse season is here again! The lunar eclipse in Pisces arrives on the 7th, and you're likely to feel it in a *major* way. If you haven't been asserting yourself, this eclipse may demand that you step up and take ownership of your own life.

Then the solar eclipse in Virgo arrives on the 21st to open the door once more to new relationships and rekindled connections. You're likely to be surprised by who walks into your life under this eclipse: the best thing to do is stay open.

Power Days

The 8th might not be the most fun day, but it's an *excellent* day for tending to your responsibilities and building the life you want. The 12th might be a good day for interviews, negotiations, and signing contracts. If you're faced with problems at work on the 26th, unconventional solutions could yield amazing results.

Days to Watch For

You probably won't be especially focused or motivated on the 6th, so try to avoid scheduling important tasks, meetings, or events.

On the 14th, avoid the temptation to jump to conclusions about what others are thinking—just ask them. On the 20th, try to stay open to changes in your close relationships, even if you don't feel ready.

October

Mercury moves into Scorpio on the 6th, followed by the Sun on the 22nd. This means that one of the best ways for you to spend this month—especially the days between the 22nd and 29th—is by doing things that expand your horizons. This could mean travel (especially to new places), signing up for a class or training program, making connections with new people, or simply reading a lot. Your mind is sharp and curious right now, and might even be a little restless, so try something new!

Moon Cycles

On the 6th, the Full Moon in Aries illuminates what is most important to you. This is a time for you to put your money where your mouth is—to commit to what you care about, knowing that doing so will make your life better overall.

Then on the 21st, the New Moon in Libra is an ideal time to take control of your financial life. Don't wait around for money to fall into your lap or count on someone else to make the tough decisions. Trust that *you* are capable of managing things.

♓

Power Days

Set aside some time to care for loved ones on the 5th: it's likely that others will come to you, and being generous with your time will benefit everyone, including you. Interviews, meetings, or presentations on the 8th should go *very* well. The 17th is a good day for taking a trip—or making future travel plans.

Days to Watch For

It will be easy to accidentally hurt others' feelings on the 16th, so be aware of the potential for misunderstandings. On the 26th, you may read way too much into coworkers' and bosses' behavior toward you—don't try to be a mind reader! Your head and your heart may be out of alignment on the 31st: ask for advice if you need it.

November

The third and final Mercury retrograde of the year is here, lasting from the 9th to the 29th. You may experience some drama with coworkers or misunderstandings with your boss between the 11th and 18th, and you're likelier than usual to make mistakes right now, so take your time and double-check your work! Then, between the 18th and 29th, Mercury retrograde may result in snags with travel—so if you're going somewhere, make sure to build in extra time for possible delays (and buy refundable tickets if you can, just in case!).

Moon Cycles

On the 5th, the Taurus Full Moon could potentially feel a bit overwhelming: there are *so* many tasks demanding your attention right now! For you, the key is to be stubborn about prioritizing: you can't do *everything*, so focus on what's important.

Then on the 20th, the Scorpio New Moon calls you to new adventures. If you're life's gotten a bit boring, or if you're just dissatisfied with where things are going, now is your time to start dreaming and planning ways to change things up.

Power Days

Luck is on your side on the 2nd, so don't be afraid to go after what you want. The 20th brings a flash of inspiration, a deepening of your intuition, or a whole new way of looking at the world. Express yourself creatively on the 29th, and don't be afraid to let your feelings show.

Days to Watch For

Past resentments may reemerge on the 4th, especially if you've felt stifled or held back by other people: focus on your future, not the past. The 13th probably isn't the best day for tough conversations—for best results, wait a couple of days. Set some time aside to deal with interpersonal issues at work on the 28th!

♓

December

As the month begins, the Sun, Venus, and Mars are all in Sagittarius and your solar tenth house of career, and Mercury joins them on the 11th. This is a perfect time for making plans, setting career goals, and having big conversations with your boss or mentor about what's next for you. Then the planets begin moving into Capricorn (Mars on the 15th, the Sun on the 21st, and Venus on the 24th). The conditions are right now for socializing, doing group activities, and building connections with others.

Moon Cycles

On the 4th, the Gemini Full Moon is an especially important one for you. There's a chance of arguments with family or roommates, but there's also a chance of surprising moments of connection with the people you live with. You may even discover secrets about your family or background.

And finally, on the 19th, the Sagittarius New Moon may bring big career news your way! Especially if you've been trying to make a change of some kind, like moving into a different role or a different industry entirely, there's a good chance you'll hear news or receive unexpected opportunities.

Power Days

Things may not go the way you planned on the 12th—but they'll probably go even better. Invest in your friendships on the 25th: don't hesitate to tell your friends how much you care about them! The 26th is a great day for making plans and setting intentions for the year ahead.

Days to Watch For

Expect some frustration on the 8th, especially when it comes to your career. Listen to this feeling: it can help you figure out where you want to go from here. You may be extra irritable with your partner on the 11th, but focus on staying kind. On the 20th, avoid the temptation to apologize for what isn't your fault.

♓

Astrology Basics

by Kim Rogers-Gallagher

The Birth Chart

Natal astrology is done by freeze-framing the solar system at the moment of your birth, from the perspective of your birthplace. This creates a circular map that looks like a pie sliced into twelve pieces. It shows where every heavenly body we're capable of seeing was located when you arrived. Basically, it's your astrological tool kit, and it can't be replicated more than once in thousands of years. This is why we astrologers are so darn insistent about the need for you to either dig your birth certificate out of that box of ancient paperwork in the back of your closet or get a copy of it from the county clerk's office where you were born. (This USA-Gov website has links to the vital records office of every state and territory: https://www.usa.gov/birth-certificate.)

Natal astrology, as interpreted by a professional astrologer, is done exactly and precisely for you and no one else. It shows your inherent traits, talents, and challenges. Comparing the planets' current positions to their positions in your birth chart allows astrologers to help you understand the celestial trends at work in your life—and most importantly, how you can put each astrological energy to a positive, productive use.

Let's take a look at the four main components of every astrology chart:

Planets: The planets represent the needs or urges we all experience once we hop off the Evolutionary

Express and take up residence inside a human body. For example, the Sun is your urge to shine and be creative, the Moon is your need to express emotions, Mercury is in charge of how you communicate and navigate, and Venus is all about who and what you love—and, more importantly, how you love.

Signs: The sign a planet occupies is like a costume or uniform. It describes how you'll go about acting on your needs and urges. If you have Venus in fiery, impulsive Aries, for example, and you're attracted to a complete stranger across the room, you won't wait for them to come to you. You'll walk over and introduce yourself the second the urge strikes you. Venus in intense, sexy Scorpio, however? Well, that's a different story. In this case, you'll keep looking at a prospective beloved until they finally give in, cross the room, and beg you to explain why you've been staring at them for the past couple of hours.

Houses: The houses represent the different sides of our personalities that emerge in different life situations. For example, think of how very different you act when you're with an authority figure as opposed to how you act with a lover or when you're with your BFF.

Aspects: The aspects describe the distance from one planet to another in a geometric angle. If you were born when Mercury was 90 degrees from Jupiter, for example, this aspect is called a square. Each unique angular relationship causes the planets involved to interact differently.

The Planets

The planets represent energy sources. The Sun is our source of creativity, the Moon is our emotional warehouse, and Venus describes who and what we love and are attracted to—not to mention why and how we go about getting it and keeping it.

Sun

The Sun is the boss in your chart. It represents your life's mission—what will give you joy, keep you young, and never fail to arouse your curiosity. Oddly enough, you weren't born knowing the qualities of the sign the Sun was in when you were born. You're here to learn the traits, talents, and characteristics of the sign you chose—and rest assured, each of the twelve is its own marvelous adventure! Since the Sun is the Big Boss, all of the other planets, including the Moon, are the Sun's staff, all there to help the boss by helping you master your particular area of expertise. Back in the day, the words from a song in a recruitment commercial struck me as a perfect way to describe our Sun's quest: "Be all that you can be. Keep on reaching. Keep on growing. Find your future." The accompanying music was energizing, robust, and exciting, full of anticipation and eagerness. When you feel enthused, motivated, and stimulated, that's your Sun letting you know you're on the right path.

Moon

If you want to understand this lovely silver orb, go outside when the Moon is nice and full, find yourself a comfy perch, sit still, and have a nice long look at it. The Moon inspires us to dream, wish, and sigh, to reminisce, ruminate, and remember. It's the Queen of Emotions, the astrological purveyor of feelings and reactions. In your natal chart, the condition of the Moon—that is, the sign and house it's in and the connections it makes with your other planets—shows how you'll deal with whatever life tosses your way: how you'll respond, how you'll cope, and how you'll pull it all together to move on after a crisis. It's where your instincts and hunches come from, and the source of every gut feeling and premonition. The Moon describes your childhood home, your relationship with your mother, your attitude toward childbearing and children in general, and what you're looking for in a home. It shows what makes you feel safe, warm, comfy, and loved. On a daily basis, the Moon describes the collective mood.

Mercury

Next time you pass by a flower shop, take a look at the FTD logo by the door. That fellow with the wings on his cap and his feet is Mercury, the ancient Messenger of the Gods. He's always been a very busy guy. Back in the day, his job was to shuttle messages back and forth between the gods and goddesses and we mere mortals—obviously, no easy feat. Nowadays, however, Mercury is even busier. With computers, cell phones, social media, and perhaps even the occasional human-to-human interaction to keep track of—well, he must be just exhausted!

In a nutshell, Mercury is the astrological energy in charge of communication, navigation, and travel, so he's still nicely represented by that winged image. He's also the guy in charge of the five senses, so no matter what you're aware of right now, be it taste, touch, sound, smell, or sight—well, that's because Mercury is bringing it to you, live. At any rate, you'll hear about him most when someone mentions that Mercury is retrograde, but even though these periods have come to be blamed for all sorts of problems, there's really no cause for alarm. Mercury turns retrograde (or, basically, appears to move backward from our perspective here on Earth) every three months for three weeks at a time, giving us all a chance for a do-over—and who among us has never needed one of those?

Venus

So, if it's Mercury that makes you aware of your environment, who allows you to experience all kinds of sensory sensations via the five senses? Who's in charge of your preferences in each department? That delightful task falls under the jurisdiction of the lovely lady Venus, who describes the physical experiences that are the absolute best—in your book, anyway. That goes for the music and art you find most pleasing, the food and beverages you can't get enough of, and the scents you consider the sweetest of all—including the collar of the shirt your loved one recently wore. Touch, of course, is also a sense that can be quite delightful to experience. Think of how happy your fingers are when you're stroking your animal companion's fur, or the delicious feel of cool bedsheets when you slip between them after an especially tough day. Venus brings all those sensations together in one wonderful package, working her magic through love of the romantic kind, most memorably experienced through intimate physical interaction with an "other." Still, your preferences in any relationship also fall under Venus's job description.

Mars

Mars turns up the heat, amps up the energy, and gets your show on the road. Whenever you hear yourself grunt, growl, or grumble—or just make any old *rrrrr* sound in general—your natal Mars has just made an appearance. Adrenaline is his business and passion is his specialty. He's the ancient God of War—a hot-headed guy who's famous for having at it with his sword first and asking questions later. In the extreme, Mars is often in the neighborhood when violent events occur, and accidents, too. He's in charge of self-assertion, aggression, and pursuit, and one glance at his heavenly appearance explains why. He's the Red Planet, after all—and just think of all the expressions about anger and passion that include references to the color red or the element of fire: "Grrr!" "Seeing red." "Hot under the collar." "All fired up." "Hot and heavy." You get the idea. Mars is your own personal warrior. He describes how you'll react when you're threatened, excited, or angry.

Jupiter

Santa Claus. Luciano Pavarotti with a great big smile on his face as he belted out an amazing aria. Your favorite uncle who drinks too much, eats too much, and laughs far too loud—yet never fails to go well above and beyond the call of duty for you when you need him. They're all perfect examples of Jupiter, the King of the Gods, the giver of all things good, and the source of extravagance, generosity, excess, and benevolence in our little corner of the universe. He and Venus are the heavens' two most popular planets—for obvious reasons. Venus makes us feel good. Jupiter makes us feel absolutely over-the-top excellent. In Jupiter's book, if one is good, it only stands to reason that two would be better, and following that logic, ten would be just outstanding. His favorite words are "too," "many," and "much." Expansions, increases, and enlargements—or basically, just the whole concept of growth—are all his doing. Now, unbeknownst to this merry old fellow, there really is such a thing as too much of a good thing—but let's not pop his goodhearted bubble. Wherever Jupiter is in your chart, you'll be prone to go overboard, take it to the limit, and push the envelope as far as you possibly can. Sure, you might get a bit out of control every now and then, but if envelopes weren't ever pushed, we'd never know the joys of optimism, generosity, or sudden, contagious bursts of laughter.

Saturn

Jupiter expands. Saturn contracts. Jupiter encourages growth. Saturn, on the other hand, uses those rings he's so famous for to restrict growth. His favorite word is "no," but he's also very fond of "wait," "stop," "not yet," and "don't even think about it." He's ultra-realistic and cautious, an exacting taskmaster who guards and protects you by not allowing you to move too quickly or act too recklessly. He insists on preparation and doesn't take kindly when we blow off responsibilities and duties. As you can imagine, Saturn is not nearly as popular as Venus and Jupiter, mainly because none of us like to be told we can't do what we want to do when we want to do it. Still, without someone who acted out his part when you were too young to know better, you might have dashed across the street without stopping to check for traffic first, and—well, you get the point.

Saturn encourages frugality, moderation, thoughtfulness, and self-restraint, all necessary habits to learn if you want to play nice with the other grown-ups. He's also quite fond of building things, which necessarily starts with solid foundations and structures that are built to last. Saturn teaches us discipline, determination, and resilience—qualities we need to actually manifest things in the real world and make our dreams come true.

Uranus

Say hello to Mr. Unpredictable himself, the heavens' wild card—to say the very least. He's the kind of guy who claims responsibility for lightning strikes, be they literal or symbolic. Winning the lottery, love at first sight, strokes of genius, accidents, and anything seemingly coincidental that strikes you as oddly well-timed are all examples of Uranus's handiwork. Uranus is a visionary, with his eye on the future and what could be. He's a rebellious, headstrong energy, so wherever he is in your chart, you'll be defiant and quite unwilling to play by the rules, which he thinks of as merely annoying suggestions that far too many humans adhere to. Uranus is here to inspire you to be yourself—exactly as you are, with no explanations and no apologies whatsoever. He motivates you to develop qualities such as independence, ingenuity, and individuality—and with this guy in the neighborhood, if anyone or anything gets in the way, you'll 86 them. Period. Buh-bye now. The good news is that when you allow this freedom-loving energy to guide you, you discover something new and exciting about yourself on a daily basis—at least. The tough but entirely doable part is keeping him reined in tightly enough to earn your daily bread and form lasting relationships with like-minded others.

Neptune

Neptune is the uncontested Mistress of Disguise and Illusion in the solar system. Just take a look at the qualities she bestows: compassion, spirituality, intuition, wistfulness, and nostalgia. Basically, whenever your subconscious whispers, it's in Neptune's voice. She activates your antennae and sends you subtle, invisible, and yet highly powerful messages about everyone you cross paths with, no matter how fleeting the encounter. I often picture her as Glinda the Good Witch from *The Wizard of Oz*, who rode around in a pink bubble, singing happy little songs and casting wonderful, helpful spells. Think "enchantment"—oh, and "glamour," too, which, by the way, was the old-time term for a magical spell cast upon someone to change their appearance. Nowadays, glamour is often thought of as a rather idealized and often artificial type of beauty brought about by cosmetics and airbrushing, but Neptune is still in charge, and her magic still works. When this energy is wrongfully used, deceptions, delusions, and fraud can result—and since she's so fond of ditching reality, it's easy to become a bit too fond of escape hatches like drugs and alcohol. Still, Neptune inspires romance, creativity, nostalgia, and sentimentality, and she's quite fond of dreams and fantasies, too—and what would life be like without all of that?

Pluto

Picture all the gods and goddesses in the heavens above us living happily in a huge mansion in the clouds. Then imagine that Pluto's place is at the bottom of the cellar stairs, and on the cellar door (which is in the kitchen, of course) a sign reads "Keep out. Working on Darwin Awards." That's where Pluto would live—and that's the attitude he'd have. He's in charge of unseen cycles—life, death, and rebirth. Obviously, he's not an emotional kind of guy. Whatever Pluto initiates really has to happen. He's dark, deep, and mysterious—and inevitable. So, yes, Darth Vader does come to mind, if for no other reason than because of James Earl Jones's amazing, compelling voice. Still, this intense, penetrating, and oh-so-thorough energy has a lot more to offer. Pluto's in charge of all those categories we humans aren't fond of—like death and decay, for example—but on the less drastic side, he also inspires recycling, repurposing, and reusing.

In your chart, Pluto represents a place where you'll be ready to go big or go home, where investing all or nothing is a given. This planet seeks to eliminate what is no longer needed to make room for something new and better. When a crisis comes up— when you need to be totally committed and totally authentic to who you really are to navigate it—that's when you'll meet your Pluto. Power struggles and mind games, however—well, you can also expect those pesky types of things wherever Pluto is located.

A Word about Retrogrades

"Retrograde" sounds like a bad thing, but I'm here to tell you that it isn't. In a nutshell, retrograde means that from our perspective here on Earth, a planet appears to be moving in reverse. It's like when you're in a moving vehicle and passing a slower car, and the other car appears to be moving backward from your point of view. Of course, planets don't ever actually back up, but the energy of retrograde planets is often held back, delayed, or hindered in some way. For example, when Mercury—the ruler of communication and navigation—appears to be retrograde, it can be tough to get from point A to point B without a snafu, and it can be equally hard to get a straight answer. Things just don't seem to go as planned. But it only makes sense. Since Mercury is the planet in charge of conversation and movement, when he's moving backward—well, imagine driving a car that only had reverse. Yep. It wouldn't be easy. Still, if that's all you had to work with, you'd eventually find a way to get where you wanted to go. That's how all retrograde energies work.

If you have retrograde planets in your natal chart, don't rush them. These energies may need a bit more time to function well for you than other natal planets, but if you're patient, talk about having an edge! You'll know these planets inside and out. On a collective basis, think of the time when a planet moves retrograde as a chance for a celestial do-over. Take advantage of this downtime to redo, reconnect, revisit, research, and reorganize.

The Signs

The sign a planet is "wearing" really says it all. It's the costume an actor wears that helps them act out the role they're playing. It's the style, manner, or approach you'll use in each life department—whether you're being creative on a canvas, gushing over a new lover, or applying for a new position. Each sign is associated with an element and a quality, as follows:

Elements: The four elements—fire, earth, air, and water—describe a sign's aims. Fire signs are spiritual, impulsive energies. Earth signs are tightly connected to the material plane. Air signs are cerebral, intellectual creatures, and water signs rule the emotional side of life.

Qualities: The three qualities—cardinal, fixed, and mutable—describe a sign's energy. Cardinal signs (Aries, Cancer, Libra, and Capricorn) are tailor-made for beginnings. Fixed signs (Taurus, Leo, Scorpio, and Aquarius) are solid, just as they sound, and are quite determined to finish what they start. Mutable signs (Gemini, Virgo, Sagittarius, and Pisces) are flexible and accommodating.

Sequence	Sign	Glyph	Ruling Planet	Symbol
1	Aries	♈	Mars	Ram
2	Taurus	♉	Venus	Bull
3	Gemini	♊	Mercury	Twins
4	Cancer	♋	Moon	Crab
5	Leo	♌	Sun	Lion
6	Virgo	♍	Mercury	Virgin
7	Libra	♎	Venus	Scales
8	Scorpio	♏	Pluto	Scorpion
9	Sagittarius	♐	Jupiter	Archer
10	Capricorn	♑	Saturn	Goat
11	Aquarius	♒	Uranus	Water Bearer
12	Pisces	♓	Neptune	Fishes

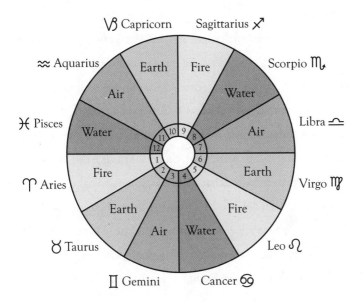

Aries

Aries is ruled by Mars and is cardinal fire—red-hot, impulsive, and ready to go. Aries planets are not known for their patience, and they ignore obstacles, choosing instead to focus on the shortest distance between where they are and where they want to be. Planets in Aries are brave, impetuous, and direct. Aries planets are often very good at initiating projects. They are not, however, as eager to finish, so they will leave projects undone. Aries planets need physical outlets for their considerable Mars-powered energy, or else their need for action can turn to stress. Exercise, hard work, and competition are food for Aries energy.

Taurus

Taurus, the fixed earth sign, has endless patience that turns your Taurus planets into a solid force to be reckoned with. Taurus folks never, ever quit. Their reputation for stubbornness is earned. They're responsible, reliable, honest as they come, practical, and endowed with a stick-to-it attitude other planets envy. They're not afraid to work hard. Since Taurus is ruled by Venus, it's not surprising to find that these people are sensual and luxury-loving, too. They love to be spoiled with the best—good food, fine wine, or even a Renoir painting. They need peace and quiet and don't like their schedules to be disrupted, but they may need a reminder that comfortable habits can become ruts.

Gemini

This sign is famous for its love of new experiences as well as its role as a communicator. Gemini is mutable air, which translates to changing your mind, so expect your Gemini planets to be entertaining and versatile. This sign knows a bit about everything. Gemini planets usually display at least two distinct sides to their personalities, are changeable and even fickle at times, and are wonderfully curious. This sign is ruled by Mercury, so if what you're doing involves talking, writing, or working with hand-eye coordination, your Gemini planets will love it. Mercury also rules short trips, so any planet in Gemini is an expert at making its way around the neighborhood in record time.

Cancer

Cancer is cardinal water, so it's good at beginning things, like emotions and families. It's also the most privacy-oriented sign. Cancer types are emotionally vulnerable, sensitive, and easily hurt. They need safe "nests" to return to when the world gets to be too much. Cancer types say "I love you" by tending to your need for food, warmth, or a place to sleep. The problem is that they can become needy, dependent, or unable to function unless they feel someone or something needs them. Cancer rules the home and family. It's also in charge of emotions, so expect a Cancer to operate from their gut most of the time.

Leo

This fixed sign is part of the fire family. As fires go, think of Leo planets as bonfires of energy—and just try to tear your eyes away. As the Lion of the zodiac, Leo cares very much about their familial pride—and about their personal pride. Sun-ruled Leo wants to shine and be noticed. Natural performers, people of this sign are into drama and attract attention even when they don't necessarily want it. Occasionally your Leo friends may be touchy and high-maintenance. Still, they are generous to a fault. Leo appreciates attention and praise with lavish compliments, lovely gifts, and creative outings designed to amaze and delight. Leo's specialties are having fun, entertaining, and making big entrances and exits.

Virgo

Virgo is called "picky" and "critical," but there is another side to this sign. More than anything, Virgo delights in helping, and since this is a mutable earth sign, it's willing to adapt to any task. Although it's true that Virgo is born with an automatic fault-finder, it's Mercury-ruled, and it's the sign with the keenest eye of all for details. When Virgo's eye for detail combines with the ability to fix almost anything, you have a troubleshooter extraordinaire. This sign practices discrimination—analyzing, critiquing, and suggesting remedies to potential problems. Virgo is also wonderful at making lists, agendas, and schedules. Keep your Virgo planets happy by keeping them busy.

Libra

Libra is affiliated with balance and harmony, both of which require an entity to give and take equally—no easy task. But no sign is more charming and sociable, or more able to coax the same qualities out of others. Libra is cardinal air, so it wants to start something that's intellectual in nature, like a conversation. Venus-ruled Libra planets are experts at behavior that is pleasing to others, so they specialize in manners, courtesy, and small talk. They don't want to be alone, and because they're gifted with the ability to pacify, they may sell out their own needs or the truth to buy peace and companionship. Their real work is to see both sides of a situation, weigh the options, and maintain their inner balance by remaining honest.

Scorpio

Planets in this sign are detectives, excelling at the art of strategy. Your Scorpio planets sift through every situation for subtle clues and then analyze them to determine what's really going on. They're also gifted at sending subtle signals back to the environment, and at imperceptibly altering a situation by manipulating it with the right word or movement. Scorpio planets are constantly searching for intimacy. They seek intensity and may be crisis-oriented. They can be relentless, obsessive, and jealous. Remember, this is fixed water. Scorpio feels things deeply and forever. Give your Scorpio planets the opportunity to fire-walk, to experience life-and-death situations.

Sagittarius

The enthusiasm of this mutable fire sign, ruled by Jupiter, spreads like a brush fire. These planets tend to never feel satisfied or content and to always wonder if there's something even more wonderful over the next mountain. Your Sagittarius planets are bored by routine; they're freedom-oriented, generous, and optimistic to a fault. They can be excessive and overindulgent. They adore foreign places and people and outdoor activities, and learn by first having the big picture explained. They're only too happy to preach and philosophize. Sagittarians can be quite prophetic, and they absolutely believe in the power of laughter—embarrassing themselves at times to make others laugh.

Capricorn

Planets in Capricorn, the cardinal earth sign ruled by Saturn, have a tendency to build things, erecting structures and creating a career for you. They will start up an organization and turn it into the family business. These planets automatically know how to run it, no matter what "it" is. They're authority figures. They exercise caution and discipline, and set down rules and live by them. Capricorn is the sign with the driest wit. Here is where your sense of propriety and tradition will be strong, where doing things the old-fashioned way and paying respect to the elders will be the only way to go. Capricorn planets want a return on the time they invest and don't mind proving how valuable they are.

Aquarius

This sign, ruled by Uranus, brings us the unpredictable. Aquarius is always ready to shock and amaze the masses and rebel against what others are doing. Planets in this sign are into personal freedom like no other. They create their own rules, fight city hall whenever possible, and deliberately break tradition. They adore change. Abrupt reversals are their specialty, so others often perceive them as erratic, unstable, or unreliable. As changeable as it seems to be, Aquarius is a fixed air sign, so when it commits to a cause or an intellectual ideal, it's really committed. Aquarius planets are often much better at friendship than love, and value being with like-minded folks.

Pisces

Watery Pisces runs on its emotions—and even more so on its intuition, which is second to none. This mutable sign can't separate itself emotionally from whatever it's exposed to. While this is the source of its well-deserved reputation for compassion, it's also the source of its desire to escape reality. Planets in Pisces feel everything—for better or worse—so they need time alone. Here is where you may have a tendency to take in stray people and animals, and where you'll need to watch for the possibility of being taken advantage of. Pisces planets see the best in a person or situation, and when reality steps in, they sometimes are disappointed. These planets are the romantics of the zodiac and often possess visionary artistic ability.

The Houses

The astrological houses are represented by the twelve pie-shaped wedges in a horoscope chart. They reflect the circumstances we create and encounter in life. They're like rooms in a house. There's a room where you keep the side of you reserved for work, another where you keep the charming, romantic lover in you, and so on. The sign on the cusp of each house—that is, the sign that appears alongside the line that precedes a house—is like the door to that "room." This sign influences the type of behavior you'll exhibit when those life circumstances turn up.

Since the signs on the house cusps are determined by the time of day you were born, it's important to have an accurate birth time when having a chart erected.

First House and Your Rising Sign

The first house shows the sign that was ascending over the horizon at the moment you were born. Let's think again of your chart as one big house and of the twelve houses as rooms. The first house is your symbolic front door. It relates to the first impression you make on people. The sign on this house cusp (a.k.a. the rising sign, or Ascendant) describes the way you dress, move, and adorn yourself, and the overall condition of your body and your health.

Second House

The second house shows how you handle the possessions you hold dear. That goes for money, objects, and qualities you value in yourself and in others. This house shows how you take care of what you have and what you buy for yourself, and the amount of money you earn. The second house shows what you're willing to do for money, too, and it's also a description of your self-esteem.

Third House

The third house corresponds to your neighborhood, including the bank, post office, and the gym where you work out. This is the side of you that performs routine tasks without much conscious thought. This house also refers to childhood and grammar school, and it shows your relationships with siblings and your communication style. It's also related to short-distance travel.

Fourth House

The fourth house is your symbolic foundation and describes your childhood home, your family of origin, and the parent who nurtured you. Here is where you'll find the part of you that decorates and maintains your nest. It describes what your home in the adult world will be like and how much privacy you'll need. It deals with real estate matters. Most importantly, this house contains the emotional warehouse of memories you operate from subconsciously.

Fifth House

The fifth house reflects the side of you that's reserved for play, that only comes out when work is done and it's time to party and be entertained. This is the charming, creative, delightful side of you. This house is where your hobbies, interests, and playmates are found. If it gives you joy, it's described here. Your fifth house shines when you are creative, and it allows you to see a bit of yourself in those creations—anything from a child's smile to a piece of art. This house is also connected to speculation and gambling.

Sixth House

The sixth house is where you keep the side of you that decides how you like things to go over the course of a day. Since it describes the duties you perform on a daily basis, this house also refers to the nature of your work, your work environment, and your coworkers. If you are the boss, this house describes your employees. The sixth house describes how you take care of your health and is related to nutrition, exercise, and fitness. Pets are also traditionally a sixth house issue since we tend to them daily and incorporate them into our routine.

Seventh House

Although the seventh house is traditionally known as the house of marriage, partnerships, and open enemies, it really holds the side of you that only comes out when you're in the company of just one other person. This is the side of you that handles relating to others on a one-to-one basis. Whenever you use the word "my" to describe your relationship with another, it's this side of you talking.

Eighth House

The eighth house reflects the crisis expert side of you that emerges when it's time to handle extreme circumstances. This is the side of you that deals with agony and ecstasy, with sex, death, and all manner of mergers, financial and otherwise. This house also holds information on surgeries, psychotherapy, and the way we regenerate and rejuvenate after loss.

Ninth House

The ninth house reflects the side of you that handles new experiences, foreign places, long-distance travel, and legal matters. Higher education, publishing, advertising, and forming opinions are all handled here, as are issues involving the big picture, such as politics, religion, and philosophy.

Tenth House

This spot in your chart describes what the public knows about you. Your career, reputation, and social status are found in the tenth house. This is the side of you that takes time to learn and become accomplished. It describes the behavior you'll exhibit when you're in charge, and also the way you'll be in the presence of an authority figure. This house describes your vocation or life's work—whatever you consider to be your "calling."

Eleventh House

Here in the eleventh house is the team player in you, the side of you that helps you find your peer groups. This house shows the type of organizations you're drawn to join, the kind of folks you consider kindred spirits, and how you'll act in group situations. It also shows the causes and social activities that you hold near and dear.

Twelfth House

The twelfth house reflects the side of you that only comes out when you're alone or in the mood to retreat and regroup. Here is where the secret side of you lives, where secret affairs and dealings take place. Here, too, is where matters like hospital stays are handled. Most importantly, this is the place where you keep all traits and behaviors you were taught early on to stifle, avoid, or deny—especially in public. This side of you is very fond of fantasy, illusion, and pretend play.

Aspects

Astrological aspects describe the relationships between planets and important points in a chart. Basically, they're the mathematical angles that measure the distance between two or more planets. Planets in square aspect are 90 degrees apart, planets in opposition are 180 degrees apart, and so forth. Each of these aspect relationships seems to link energies in a very different way. For example, if two planets are in square aspect, think of what you know about "squaring off," and you'll understand exactly how they're interacting. Think of aspects as a way of describing the type of conversation going on between celestial bodies.

Here is a brief description of the five major aspects.

Conjunction

When two planets are within a few degrees of each other, they're joined at the hip. The conjunction is often called the aspect of "fusion," since the energies involved always act together.

Sextile

Planets in sextile are linked by a 60-degree angle, creating an exciting, stimulating astrological "conversation." These planets encourage, arouse, and excite each other.

Square

The square aspect is created by linking energies in a 90-degree angle—which tends to be testy and sometimes irritating but always action-oriented.

Trine

The trine is the "lazy" aspect. When planets are in this 120-degree angle, they get along so well that they often aren't motivated to do much. Trines make things easy—too easy, at times—but they're also known for being quite lucky.

Opposition

Oppositions exist between planets that are literally opposite each other. Think about seesaws and playing tug-of-war, and you'll understand how these energies get along. Sure, it can be a power struggle at times, but balance is the key.

Kim Rogers-Gallagher has written hundreds of articles and columns for magazines and online publications and has two books of her own, *Astrology for the Light Side of the Brain* and *Astrology for the Light Side of the Future*. She's a well-known speaker who's been part of the UAC faculty since 1996. Kim can be contacted at KRGPhoenix313@yahoo.com for fees regarding readings, classes, and lectures.